Nelson Mandela

A life in cartoons

edited by

Harry Dugmore
Stephen Francis
Rico Schacherl

ANGLOVAAL ● MINING
AVMIN

David Philip Publishers

Thanks to Dov Fedler, Zapiro, Dr. Jack, Derek Bauer and Tom Halliday
for permission to use their cartoons on the cover of this book.
Thanks to Karina Turok for permission to use her photograph of
Nelson Mandela on the back cover of this book.

Published in 1999 in Southern Africa by
David Philip Publishers (Pty) Ltd
208 Werdmuller Centre, Claremont 7708
in association with Rapid Phase (Pty) Ltd
Johannesburg

ISBN 0-86486-393-4 (Soft cover)

ISBN 086486-457-4 (Hard cover)

Reproduction by Syreline Process
Printed by CTP Book Printers, Caxton Street, Parow, Cape.

Zapiro

Acknowledgements

In compiling a book such as this, we've accumulated many debts of gratitude to people and institutions who have helped, instructed and inspired us along the way.

Gulietta Fafak worked unflaggingly to track cartoons and cartoonists from every corner of the globe. Her attention to detail and can-do attitude made this work possible.

Zann Hoad, who oversaw the publishing process from its inception, has shown that she has few peers when it comes to drive and determination. Her cheerful attitude kept the book moving forward.

Zapiro, aka Jonathan Shapiro, provided encouragement, leads and inspiration. His cartoons are some of the finest in this book, and his help and support are greatly appreciated.

David and Marie Philip, and Bridget Impey, Russell Martin, Francois van Schalkwyk and Maggie Davey at David Philip Publishers have been enthusiastic supporters of this project from the beginning. They have had to put up with maverick suggestions and unusual methodologies. No one could hope for a more cheerful publishing partner, or one more committed to the freeing of human potential.

Ryan Francois and Ardi Schutz have worked on the design, the cover and the look and feel of this book. Their artistry makes this book easy on the eye, and gives proper weight to the art of the cartoonists.

Many friends and academic colleagues commented on various chapters of this book. Charles Dugmore, a dedicated historian, checked facts, proofed drafts and provided clear analysis when it was needed most. Joey Monson's research was impeccable and her sense of organisation helped get the initial 2000 cartoons down to the 166 of the very best which are included in this book. Steve Kromberg and Erica Elk have supported the project from its inception and always provided the most constructive kind of feedback.

Gail Strauss inspired this book's genesis with warmth, affection and well-timed criticism. Lindsey Stevens at Rapid Phase provided the back-up and support necessary to complete this book – and so many other projects. Her sense of humour brought us through the many fearsome deadlines. Indeed everyone at Rapid Phase, and our parent company, New Africa Investments Limited (NAIL), has made this publication possible.

Each cartoonist represented in this book has something to say. Usually its something funny, or something thought-provoking. Often their cartoons are moving and poignant. The talent represented in this book is remarkable – we want to thank and acknowledge every cartoonist who made their work and their time available to us.

We particularly want to thank Archbishop Desmond Tutu for his moving forward to this book. Nadine Gordimer and Pieter-Dirk Uys generously commented on the concept of this publication.

Rick Menell, CEO of Anglovaal Mining Limited, generously sponsored the research and development of this book. Anglovaal Mining Limited continues to provide a model for corporate commitment to developing the new South Africa.

Publishing this book is our small way of expressing our thanks to Nelson Rolihlahla Mandela for his role in liberating our country, inspiring our nation, and reawakening in all of us a sense of our humanity and what we are capable of achieving.

This book is dedicated to him with love and gratitude.

Contents

Foreword

Most public relations and advertising executives would be willing to give a leg and an arm to have the product recognition associated with Nelson Mandela for whatever article they are promoting – a recognition attested to by this collection of some 166 cartoons by 54 cartoonists from around the world. Of him it could truly be said, he needs no introduction, he is so well known.

Perhaps, not entirely. You see, once when I was in San Francisco a lady accosted me and very cheerily called out, "Hello, Archbishop Mandela!" She may have been wanting two for the price of one.

Apart from this almost bizarre exception, Nelson Mandela certainly has been the most recognisable and the most sought after head of state. This is a tremendous turn-around when you think that a formidable British Prime Minister dismissed him as a "terrorist". In his own country, after eluding capture as the "Black Pimpernel", the authorities tried to turn him into a non-person. He could not be quoted; no pictures of him were allowed; and they hoped that he would disappear into the limbo of amnesia assisted by a life sentence at their top-security island prison, Robben Island.

Wonderfully for the world, nothing of the sort happened. Perversely, in the view of his jailers, his stature grew and grew until he became the world's most famous political prisoner, and from prison he seemed, like a master magician, able to transmit his spell of charm and greatness.

In 1988 I was one of the speakers at a Hyde Park Corner rally to celebrate his 70th birthday. Some 250 000 people converged on Hyde Park Corner, several thousands having walked as on a pilgrimage from the many corners of the United Kingdom. And most of that massive crowd were youngsters, many of whom had not been born when Madiba went to prison.

People feared that we would be disillusioned when he emerged from incarceration, that our idol would be found to have feet of clay. What a fantastic vindication of goodness when he emerged: all the world and her husband were glued to their TV sets because this was without exaggeration one of the defining moments of our century.

Everywhere he has been it is as if he is a kind of Pied Piper – everybody, not just children, falling under his charismatic spell. Massive crowds hang on his every word, everywhere in the world.

The paparazzi could not get enough of him. Here he was with that extraordinary willingness to forgive, with remarkable magnanimity, wearing a No. 6 Springbok jersey and driving rugby enthusiasts into a frenzy – in that one action, striking a blow for reconciliation which several speeches in a week of Sundays would not have accomplished; visiting the widow of the high priest of apartheid; and lunching with the man who had prosecuted him and his fellow accused in the Rivonia Trial. An incredible icon of reconciliation and goodness. And the world could not have enough of him.

Everyone wanted to have a photo opportunity with him – the Spice Girls, Princess Di, various heads of state and miscellaneous politicians who wanted to breathe new life into their moribund careers; the list is endless. I do not know of any other politician who has been asked to so many summit farewells, of the OAU, the Commonwealth, the EU, different countries vying to have him carry out a farewell state visit. And because of his transparent goodness and integrity, only he could have persuaded Colonel Gaddafi to hand over the Lockerbie suspects.

It is a cliché, but it is true: he is a moral giant, a colossus.

We have all been thrilled to be alive when he is around. You were proud to be a human being because of this extraordinary human being. Everyone is so happy that he has got the girl of his heart and we are thrilled that they can ride into the sunset to live happily ever after. Did I say he was well known? Well, he likes to tell this story against himself. On Robben Island he was conversing with one of the inmates and asked him why he was there. The man gave him details of his activity as a member of the ANC. Then the man turned to Madiba and asked, "Well now, what about you, why are you here?"

He is God's gift to South Africa and he is our gift to the world.

Archbishop Desmond Tutu
October 1999

Introduction

Zapiro's cartoon "Nelson Mandela, the early years", which opens this book, describes a poignantly imaginative scene: a teacher in a rural classroom comments to the headmaster about the very young Nelson Mandela: "This one can't make up his mind (what he is going to be when he grows up): Lawyer, Activist, Freedom Fighter, Prisoner of Conscience, President, Reconciler, Nation Builder, Visionary and 20th Century Icon."

Millions of words have been written about the man who was – and is – all of these personas. This book is much more about the pictures than words, or, more precisely, it is about the particularly artful combination of words and pictures, the modern political cartoon. Nelson Mandela, the most extra-ordinary South African, has inspired at least two thousand cartoons in his lifetime, and this book showcases the best of these. Fifty-four cartoonists, from more than a dozen countries, capture a part of the famed Madiba Magic with a warmth that few other mediums can match.

Finding and then selecting these cartoons proved more difficult than expected. Mandela's 27 years in apartheid jails kept him from the public eye more effectively than most might care to remember – given that he is now the most famous person in the world. Surprisingly, there are almost no cartoons dealing directly with Nelson Mandela before 1980. This reflects partly the bias of the white-owned and white-controlled mass media, and partly the effect of draconian security legislation which successive apartheid governments implemented. No images, representations or photos of Mandela were allowed from 1964 onwards. Under sections 44(e) and 44(f) of the Prisons Act (Act 8 of 1959) it was a serious criminal offence in South Africa to "cause any sketch or photograph of any prison, portion of a prison, prisoner or group of prisoners" to be published. More than a hundred other laws limited freedom of speech and freedom of the press in South Africa in some way.

But a great thaw began in the early 1980s as resistance to apartheid intensified. From about 1980, the names of the African National Congress (ANC) and its imprisoned leader were systematically revived by an energised and reorganised ANC. The formation of the Release Mandela Committee in 1981, a conspicuous part of the movement to rally support for the ANC's cause around the persona of Nelson Mandela, marked an important turning-point in the history of resistance in South Africa. From this time on Mandela re-entered the public landscape and he and the ANC started to attract more generous media coverage. The first cartoons about Nelson Mandela begin to appear at this time.

Human memory is forgiving, seeking as it does to accentuate the positive, and dull the pain of past realities.

Many of the cartoons from the pre-1990 era featured in this book have been selected to remind us of exactly how cruel the apartheid system was, and how profoundly it affected the lives of every South African. As Allister Sparks writes in *Tomorrow is Another Country*, his brilliant account of the secret negotiations which led to Mandela's release and the ANC's unbanning:

> "Slavery debases master as well as slave. The warder becomes prisoner in his own jail; he is never free from the business of oppression and confinement. So, too, in apartheid South Africa, where white and black had been bound together in a web of mutual destructiveness. Apartheid, brutalizing the whites as it destroyed the self-esteem of the blacks, robbed both of their humanity."

Nelson Mandela's singular contribution to South Africa was to return that stolen humanity to a broken nation and, in so doing, inspire the world. He restored, for many, faith in the possibility of the triumph of good over evil, and of civility over self-interest.

In 1992 we created a new political cartoon strip in South Africa, "Madam & Eve". Conjuring up a daily cartoon in a country which has transformed so quickly, has been daunting. But we have come to realise that writing comedy in the most interesting and passionate country in the world, in the most interesting and passionate time of its history, is actually a rare privilege. Living through the Nelson Mandela era continues to be invigorating, not just for us, but for all South Africans.

The three of us have also been fortunate to meet Nelson Mandela a number of times, and to have heard him commend cartoonists, both local and international, for their role in preserving freedom, exposing corruption –

and for just letting people laugh. Coming from a man who himself has the most incredible sense of humour – lightning fast, sharp and direct, hearty and sincere, self-deprecating and humble – his kind and thought-provoking words about our craft will continue to inspire cartoonists everywhere. As many cartoons in these pages show, even the most cynical hacks are allowed, sometimes, to be fans.

Harry Dugmore
Stephen Francis
Rico Schacherl
Johannesburg
October 1999

Sponsor's Message

Late in 1999 we were asked together with others to support a party hosted by Nelson Mandela in Postmasburg, a remote mining and farming town in South Africa's Northern Cape province, as part of the Nelson Mandela Celebration of Children. Thousands of children came from all over this desert territory for the great occasion. Famous people flew in from far continents to join the fun. Madiba as always greeted hundreds of adults and children personally, danced in front of a childrens' choir and brought tears and involuntary broad grins of delight to all who saw him and heard him. This was a great day for the small faraway community: the day the great Madiba, who led South Africa into the light, brought his joy and magic to town and made everyone feel more worthy, important and capable of greater things.

Later on the same day, ten miles away, Associated Manganese mines hosted a Safety Festival with competitions for many mines in the region at its Beeshoek iron ore operation. Standing watching the prize giving with the Chief Executive of the Nelson Mandela Childrens' Fund, we looked down at our feet and saw a small white boy and a slightly older black girl playing gleefully under the benign gaze of their parents amongst the very mixed and happy crowd. Our eyes met and we didn't need to speak our thoughts: those who knew this community only ten years ago with all its segregation, rigidity and fear can appreciate the miracle that has occurred in South Africa over such a short time under the inspired leadership of Nelson Mandela.

Our country has been transformed and a grim destiny has turned into a future full of promise. The most hectic and challenging years of this transformation have been its middle chapters – the nearly ten years from Nelson Mandela's release from prison in February 1990 until his gracious retirement at the inauguration of his elected successor President Thabo Mbeki in June 1999. For South Africans this will always be the Era of Nelson Mandela.

The period of transition from Apartheid to democracy has been hugely problematic. It appeared that things could have fallen apart and gone dreadfully wrong at several key junctures. For millions of South Africans living their lives day to day it has been therefore a time of great uncertainty and anxiety. Above all this turmoil stood Madiba: steadfast, clear in his values and certain of purpose, always seeking the path of reconciliation and mutual respect, daily wielding his well-earned moral stature in a canny way to recruit people from all backgrounds to serve the great mission of the party to which he has remained unswervingly loyal. His gift for symbolic gestures and robust good humour inspired a whole nation to rise above fear and anger. He helped those of us in business as well, as people in all walks of life, to define new roles and purpose. Under his leadership we triumphed and amazed the world.

There have been countless heroes in South Africa who have worked for freedom, democracy and development. There are many at work today. As a great leader, Nelson Mandela has provided both a sure compass for their collective efforts and a sense of urgency and importance to each individual's contribution. The grandfather of 23 constantly reminds all of us with both his words and his actions that the work is for the children, to whom we owe everything.

This wonderful human epic that has touched the lives of so many with inspiration, compassion and humour is captured beautifully through the medium of the cartoonist. The great cartoonists whose work fills this book highlight the essence of the story of Nelson Mandela's life so far. We are proud to be associated with this venture and proud to be South Africans who lived and worked during the Era of Nelson Mandela.

Rick Menell
Anglovaal Mining Limited
October 1999

Chapter 1

The crucible of apartheid

Moir

Nelson Mandela was born in 1918, just a few months before the carnage of World War One ended. The "war to end all wars" cost 10 million lives but did little to kill off the primary ideologies of the era: nationalism, racism and an almost universal sexism. Despite the ruin of Europe, the belief that some people – women, Jews, blacks, Asians in particular – were inherently inferior to others took on new and often more violent forms. Democracy was everywhere in its infancy, with old feudal structures of kings and queens as vigorous in Europe as they were in Africa. The European powers had divided Africa among themselves in the 19th century, and they ruled their colonies with variations of iron-handed governance. No-where in the Africa in which Mandela was born did any black African have the vote. And nowhere in the Africa of 1918 did any women have political rights; even white South African women were denied the franchise until 1930.

In the light of where the world stood when Nelson Mandela was born, his – and South Africa's achievements – by the century's end are even more remarkable. In the South Africa of 1918, whites generally agreed that blacks were inferior to whites. But two rather different strands of racial thinking competed for supremacy among the white rulers of the country. There were those who believed that black South Africans were essentially like children who could, with careful nurturing, one day "grow up" and eventually be given "civilised rights". Opposed to this view was that of other whites who believed that black Africans were inherently and permanently inferior. They could thus never be "raised" to the level of the white master race.

In the Second World War those who believed in the former fought against and triumphed over those who believed the latter. The core ideas behind the Thousand Year Reich of Hitler's Herrenvolk and the zealous racism of Hirohito's Japan – the innate superiority of a particular gene pool – were crushed by 1945. Most of the world got the message: within twenty years the European powers had given independence to the majority of their colonies.

OBSESSED WITH RACE

But South Africa would become a major exception to the new colonial consensus. The National Party won control of the South African government in a whites-only general election 1948. Many Nationalists had been ardent Nazi supporters. They were steeped in the belief that blacks were genetically inferior to whites, and that the white "race" would be compromised and its "purity" diluted by contact with blacks. Almost the first laws the National Party Government passed were the Prohibition of Mixed Marriages Act and the Immorality Act. Indeed, until the 1980s it would be a serious crime for black and white to have any kind of sexual relationship. In 1950, just two years after their election, the National Party also passed the Population Registration Act, which categorised all South Africans into rigorously defined ethnic groups.

But in the wake of the defeat of Nazi Germany and its allies, the idea of the genetic racial inferiority of some groups was becoming an anathema. By the time Nelson Mandela was in his twenties, it was becoming unacceptable to deprive blacks of land and political rights on the grounds that blacks were inferior. Coming to power in 1948 on a hard-line racist platform, promising to put "kaffirs in their place", even the Nationalists knew they would soon need a new story, a new ideology and a new grand plan.

THE CREATION OF APARTHEID

For the founders of apartheid, the solution was simple, and, so they believed, even elegant. During the 1950s, partly in response to the successful defiance campaign against racist laws led by Nelson Mandela in 1952, and partly in the face of African nationalism's successes in the rest of Africa (Ghana becoming the first independent African country in 1957), the National Party began to switch tack and embrace the more paternalistic racism which was favoured by Britain, and indeed by most English-speaking white South Africans. The South African Prime Minister, Hendrik Verwoerd, who took power in 1958, started to espouse the view that black people could in fact "grow up", and one day enjoy "adult" political rights. But there was a new and ingenious twist to this story – of course blacks could enjoy political rights – but not in South Africa. Rather create ten tribal "homelands" for all South Africa's black groups, send the Indian population back to India and consider a possible homeland for coloureds as well.

This, in essence, was Verwoerd's dream, and the ideological bedrock of what the world came to know as apartheid. This is what the ANC and Nelson Mandela were up against. Every black South African would be allocated to a "country" where they could enjoy full political rights in time – and a vote, a nationality, a flag, and a separate national anthem. Of course the citizens of these new countries could visit white South Africa – to work in the factories, mines and homes. But they had to go back to their homelands to vote and, when their usefulness to the economy was over, to die. In this vision there would eventually be, in Connie Mulder's famous words in 1978, "no black South Africans".

For white South Africa this new system had the additional benefit of creating a small black middle class working safely within the system. Each homeland would need governments, bureaucrats and officials who would have a deep material stake in preserving the system. Indeed, Mandela's closest childhood friend and relative, KD Matanzima, was an early and ardent supporter of the homeland system that underpinned apartheid.

Richard Smith

The Apartheid government would forcibly move more than three million South Africans to artificial tribal homelands. Here Piet Koornhof, the most famous minister of "plural relations" (a.k.a. the Department in charge of moving blacks around in the 1970s) speaks the double-talk that he would personally become famous for.

FANTASY AND REALITY

Grand apartheid really was a grand plan. But it was so obviously flawed that it is hard to believe that even its adherents really bought into it. Firstly, the apartheid government, following previous white minority governments, proposed giving Africans, already 87% of the population of South Africa, only 13% of the land for the ten independent homelands. In addition, the reality of the South African landscape was that millions of black South Africans resided outside the proposed areas, and would have to be removed to their appropriate ethnic homeland. To make the entire plan even more implausible, millions of black South Africans had also left their rural lands forever and were, by 1948, living in the major cities of South Africa. These second and third-generation urbanites would also have to be removed, if possible. But if this were not possible, the existing black areas of the city would be declared something akin to large "temporary holding areas". There blacks could, by permit, reside for most of the year so as to work in the white-owned factories, mines and homes.

SPARE NO EXPENSE

As contrived as these plans were, the National Party government set about trying to achieve them with a rare sense of divine mission and drive. Nelson Mandela, the ANC and other opposition groups seriously underestimated the determination of National Party zealots to make the unworkable work. By 1975, all ten ethnic homelands had been established, and millions of Africans had been forcibly removed from all over South Africa to what were deemed to be their homelands. Billions of rands were spent creating national capitals, sumptuous airports and other trappings of independence for these new countries.

We easily forget how complex, how crazy and how cruel the racism of apartheid was. The cartoons in this first chapter try to provide a sense of context, a backdrop for what Nelson Mandela and the ANC were up against. Much of it will be familiar to older South Africans, but for younger generations, and for readers less familiar with our history, the absurdity of apartheid bears a brief retelling. This is the context which caused Nelson Mandela to choose the path of liberator-in-chief. As he wrote in his autobiography, *Long Walk to Freedom*:

> "I cannot pinpoint a moment when I became politicized, when I knew that I would spend my life in the liberation struggle. I had no epiphany, no singular revelation, no moment of truth, but a steady accumulation of a thousand slights, and a thousand indignities produced in me an anger, a desire to fight the system that imprisoned my people."

Nelson Mandela would both fight and defeat this system, doing more than any other person to liberate South Africa from the inhumanity of apartheid. ꩜꩜

 This is a homeland

(actual size)

 This is a fragmented homeland

 This is a fragmented citizen of a fragmented homeland

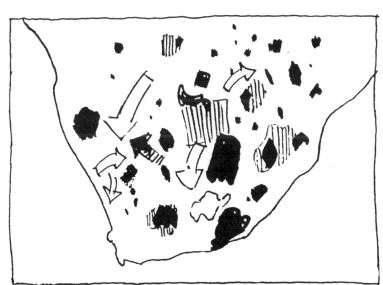

— and this, a fragmented country with fragmented homelands whose fragmented citizens develop separately in their own fragmented way....

Abe Berry, 1970

Not only did the apartheid government allocate only 13% of South Africa's total land mass for black South Africa's "homelands", the reality of the country's geography was such that only the Transkei and Ciskei homelands were in one solid geographical piece. Bophuthatswana for instance was made up of eleven separate pieces of land.

J.H. Jackson, 1959

The world, and South Africa's black population, were not fooled by the pretensions of the proposed homelands system. Mandela writes in his autobiography: "The Bantustan system had been conceived by Dr. H.F. Verwoerd, the Minister of Native Affairs, as a way of muting international criticism of South African racial policies but at the same time institutionalizing apartheid. The idea was to preserve the status quo where three million whites owned 87 per cent of the land, and relegate the eight million Africans to the remaining 13 per cent."

Richard Wilson, 1971

Grand Apartheid was ultimately based on a division of land – an extremely unfair division at that. As Mandela recalled in his autobiography: "The government's intention in creating the homeland system was to keep the Transkei – and other African areas – as reservoirs of cheap labour for white industry. At the same time, the covert goal of the goverment was to create an African middle class to blunt the appeal of the ANC and the liberation struggle."

Plantu, 1985

Gold mining has long been the mainstay of the South African economy. Leaving his rural home in the Transkei, partly to escape an arranged marriage, Mandela arrived in Johannesburg in 1941. He secured a job as a mine security officer at the Crown Mines on the outskirts of Johannesburg. He recalls in his autobiography:

"Gold mining on the Witwatersrand was costly because the ore was low grade and deep under the earth. Only cheap labour in the form of thousands of Africans working long hours for little pay made gold-mining profitable for the mining houses."

Abe Berry, 1966

So-called "petty apartheid" (named to distinguish it from "grand apartheid", which referred to the creation of separate tribal homelands) forbade different ethnic groups to share facilities. The Separate Amenities Act ensured that all South Africa's public spaces were segregated, which meant physically dividing parks, beaches and other amenities into different sections. White South Africans relied heavily on domestic workers to bring up their children – and, as Berry depicts in this cartoon, these caregivers had to take their charges to segregated facilities every day.

J. H. Jackson, 1958

By the end of the 1950s the apartheid government had passed legislation to restrict and control every aspect of black life. Mandela writes in his autobiography: "If we had any hopes or illusions about the National Party before they came into office, we were disabused of them quickly. Their threat to put the kaffir in his place was not an idle one." Here Henrick Verwoerd draws the curtain on the limited human rights South Africans experienced in the 1950s.

Bob Connolly, 1960

In the early part of 1960, the ANC made a last attempt to convince the white government that peaceful accommodation of the black majority's political aspirations was possible. The ANC called for an all-inclusive political convention – not unlike the CODESA meetings which eventually took place 31 years later. As Mandela wrote in a letter in 1960: "We have called on the Government to convene an elected National Convention of representatives of all races without delay, and to charge that Convention with the task of drawing up a new Constitution for this country which would be acceptable to all racial groups. We can see no workable alternative to this proposal, except that the Nationalist Government proceeds to enforce a minority decision on all of us, with the certain consequence of still deeper crisis, and a continuing period of strife and disaster ahead. Stated bluntly, the alternatives appear to be these: talk it out, or shoot it out." Verwoerd did not reply to Mandela's prophetic offer. Verwoerd's stature as a hard man, which he no doubt welcomed, became entrenched.

Ashton, 1960

On 21 March 1960, the police at Sharpeville opened fire on a Pan Africanist Congress (PAC) demonstration. The PAC had been formed in 1959 after a small group of "Africanists", who objected to the ANC's co-operation with anti-apartheid-minded whites and Indians, broke away from the ANC and formed their own organisation. Sixty-nine people were shot dead at Sharpeville; most were shot in the back while running away from the police.

Mandela recalled: "The shootings at Sharpeville provoked national turmoil and a government crisis. Outraged protests came in from across the globe, the Johannesburg Stock Exchange plunged, and capital started to flow out of the country. The massacre also precipitated the declaration of a State of Emergency, the banning of the ANC and the PAC, and South Africa's descent into thirty years of outright repression of black political opposition."

David Marais, 1960

By the late 1950s, the apartheid government had made a tactical decision to destroy black resistance to apartheid and to criminalise even mild criticism of apartheid inside the country. The banning of the ANC and PAC in 1960 (the Communist Party had been banned in 1950) signalled the new hard-line attitude that the National Party would become notorious for. Here, Verwoerd and other members of his cabinet drive black opposition groups underground.

Len Sak, 1961

Hardliner B.J. Vorster was made Minister of Justice by Verwoerd in 1961. In a flurry of legislative activity in the early 1960s, the apartheid government swept away the right of habeas corpus, introducing detention without trial, various forms of administrative bannings, house arrests, banishments, and a variety of other repressive measures.

"I must also caution you that anything I may say will be taken down and used as evidence against you."

Graffito (aka Peter Clarke), 1966

As the apartheid government's determination to eradicate all opposition became more apparent, cartoons like this marked the absurdity of the government's claim to respect due legal process.

Scores of anti-apartheid leaders were arrested in the early 1960s, culminating in the mass arrest of the ANC high command in 1963.

"It's not that I'm against democracy – it's just that I've never had much to with it..."

Peter Clarke, 1966

Justice Minister B.J. Vorster was interned during the Second World War for his Nazi sympathies. Vorster became Prime Minister in 1966 following the assassination of Hendrik Verwoerd. Under his ten-year tenure, South Africa would become, for all intents and purposes, a police state.

"No rent... immediate occupation... a life-long lease... the most wonderful view in the world... what more could anyone ask for?"

David Marais, 1966

The eight convicted ANC leaders narrowly escaped the death penalty for treason. Black South Africa was indeed imprisoned. And white South Africans were the jailers. Here B.J. Vorster, then Minister of Justice and later to be Prime Minister, gives what became an apartheid government mantra: Blacks in South Africa have never had it so good. What are they complaining about? Wasn't Robben Island the most beautiful prison you'd ever seen?

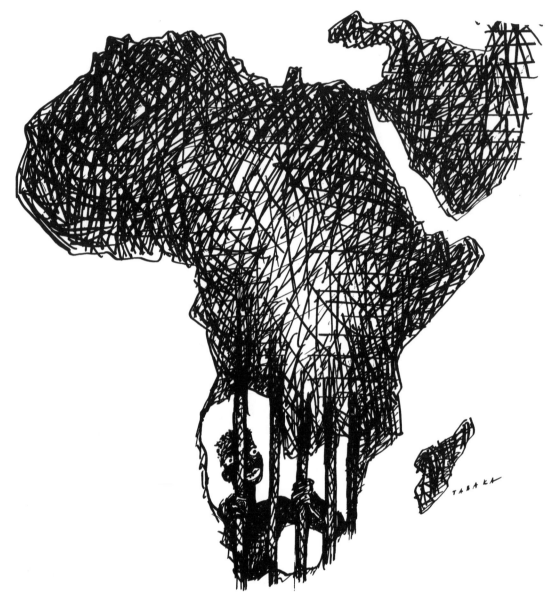

Margaret Tabaka, 1964

Nelson Mandela had been arrested in 1962 and sentenced to five years' imprisonment for leaving the country unlawfully. In 1963 almost the entire top leadership of the ANC were arrested at their secret headquarters in Rivonia, and put on trial. Nelson Mandela was brought from prison to join them as "Accused number one".

Mandela's famous four-hour speech from the dock at the conclusion of what became known as the Rivonia Trial would be the last time he was heard in public for 26 years. His closing words to the court have now become the most quoted of all his statements:

"I have fought against white domination, and I have fought against black domination. I have cherished the ideal of a democratic and free society in which all persons live together in harmony and with equal opportunities. It is an ideal which I hope to live for and to achieve. But if needs be, it is an ideal for which I am prepared to die."

Chapter 2

The long, lonely wasted years

Keith Ticehurst

The strategy of clamping down hard on the opposition seemed to have paid off for the apartheid government. By 1965 Nelson Mandela and the entire top leadership of the ANC were either in jail or in exile. In the relative calm that followed, Western countries, particularly the UK, poured money into South Africa and its economy grew faster than any other country in the world. South African all-white sports teams beat the best in the world in rugby and cricket, giving whites some reassurance of their superiority. These sporting moments were hyped to the hilt by the government and took the sting from the country being thrown out of the Olympic movement in 1964.

By the early 1970s there was almost no visible resistance to apartheid, other than small-scale protests on a few university campuses, and brave appeals to conscience from organisations like the Black Sash. Even the Liberal Party, a largely white party headed by the famous author Alan Paton, was dissolved in 1968.

But beneath the veneer of this seeming calm, all was not well in the apartheid state. While the Nationalists started to forcibly move millions of Africans to the new tribal homelands, or into new urban ghettos like Soweto, pockets of resistance were springing up both at home and abroad. The ANC began winning friends across Africa, Asia and Europe, opening up offices in dozens of countries. Highly motivated ANC cadres began to receive training in guerrilla war in Eastern bloc countries and in African states. The idea of economic sanctions began to be placed on the world's agenda.

THE WIND OF CHANGE

At home, charismatic new black leaders began to emerge, most famously Steve Biko. Biko led black students out of the largely white student organisation, NUSAS, and formed the South African Students Organisation (SASO) in the late 1960s. By 1973 the labour movement also began stirring again, and effective strikes swept Natal. Indeed, the formation of black trade unions, and later of trade union federations like FOSATU and COSATU, marked critical turning points in organised resistance in South Africa. These union bodies gave opponents of apartheid a powerful new weapon – the withdrawal of labour from the largely white-owned economy – to begin pressing the government. While the ANC-led boycotts of the 1950s had been confined to short and sharp actions, the unions held out the promise of long-term, more crippling economic action.

Jeno Dallos

In South Africa's neighbouring states, and across Africa, the wind of change predicted by British Prime Minister Harold Macmillan in 1960 was blowing with unpredicted strength. Botswana, Swaziland, Lesotho, Malawi, Kenya, Tanzania and Zambia all achieved independence by 1970. Angola and Mozambique became independent in 1975, much to the jubilation of black South Africa. Only South Africa, Namibia (then called South West Africa by the occupying South African government) and Ian Smith's Rhodesia held out as bastions of white rule in Africa by 1975.

1976 – YEAR OF FIRE, YEAR OF ASH

In June 1976, simmering tensions in black schools over the imposition of Afrikaans as a medium of instruction boiled over into mass protest. Marches were organised and although they were entirely peaceful, the South African security forces did not hesitate to use lethal force. On 16 June police opened fire on a pupils' march, killing 13-year-old Hector Petersen. This murder and others provoked a furious reaction – within three days Soweto was in full revolt. Other townships across South Africa quickly joined the uprising, and apartheid security forces would shoot dead hundreds of school children, and detain thousands more, before they restored an uneasy calm in September.

1976 was a landmark year in the history of the South African liberation struggle. The independence of the Transkei in 1976 had been an embarrassing failure for the government, as it failed to win recognition from any country in the world. The rapid spread of black resistance in 1976 had frightened the white government, and shocked the world, as images of young children being gunned down by security forces appeared regularly in foreign newspapers and on foreign television. Thousands of pupils abandoned their studies and fled the country to join the guerrilla armies of the liberation movements in exile. As Mandela recalled:

"Suddenly the young people of South Africa were fired with the spirit of protest and rebellion. Students boycotted schools all across the country. My comrades and I were enormously cheered, as there is nothing so encouraging in prison as learning that the people outside are supporting the cause for which you are inside."

BACKLASH

The National Party government was determined to regain control, no matter what the cost. In 1977 it announced that 19 organisations would be banned, and popular black newspapers such as *The World* would be forced to close down. The black consciousness movement, the inspiring philosophy which emphasised black self-reliance and black pride, and which had fuelled the 1976 uprising, was crushed. On 12 September 1977 Steve Biko, the charismatic and popular leader of SASO, was tortured to death by security police. This high-profile murder evoked condemnation and outrage from around the world. Biko was the 24th detainee to die mysteriously at the hands of the security police while under interrogation. At the Truth Commission hearings in the 1990s, the horrendous torture methods used on detainees were partly revealed. The ruthlessness of the security police, who would ultimately torture over a hundred detainees to death, remains one of the great unpunished crimes of the apartheid era.

TOTAL ONSLAUGHT

Outright repression, even that as brutal as it unleashed in 1976-78, could only provide short-term respite. From the days of Verwoerd, the Nationalist government knew that some kind of political accommodation of black aspirations would eventually have to be made. The homelands system was clearly not working. In 1978 B.J. Vorster was replaced as Prime Minister with the more reform-minded regime of

P.W. Botha and his close ally, General Magnus Malan. Realising that some bold step was needed, Botha sent signals to the world that he was ready to offer concessions, and might even free Mandela under certain strict conditions. This was, in 1978, heady stuff.

But it soon became obvious that Botha had no intention of dismantling apartheid, or of tampering with the central tenet of apartheid ideology – that there would eventually be "no black South Africans". Apartheid with a human face was the most that Botha seemed to aspire to.

ISOLATION AND HARD LABOUR

Until the advent of the Botha government in 1978, Nelson Mandela and other political prisoners were confined to Robben Island, and subject to the harshest possible regime. Like other political prisoners, Mandela was initially restricted to one thirty-minute visit every six months and was allowed to write and receive only one letter every six months. These two letters a year were heavily censored. No newspapers or radios were allowed in the prison at all; Mandela would be deprived of news until 1978 when prisoners were finally allowed heavily censored newspapers.

In his autobiography, Mandela recalls many of the cruelties inflicted upon him and his fellow prisoners during his first decade on Robben Island. His recollections of mining lime in the island's lime quarry, which he did for 13 years, give some indication of the daily indignities that the prisoners suffered:

> "The lime quarry looked like an enormous white crater cut into a rocky hillside. Warders with automatic weapons stood on raised platforms watching us. Unarmed warders walked among us, urging us to work harder. Go on! Go on!, they would shout, as if we were oxen. We worked until four, when we carted the lime to the waiting trucks. By the end of the day, our faces and bodies were caked with white dust."

Confined to the island, and placed in a cell which measured 6 feet by 8 feet, Mandela has referred to this time in prison as "the long, lonely and wasted years". In addition to the privations of prison life, he also had to endure the repeated incarceration of his wife Winnie. In 1969 Winnie was detained without trial and, in Mandela's words, "placed in solitary confinement in Pretoria, denied bail and visitors and relentlessly and brutally interrogated". This systematic torture of his wife – which prison authorities made sure that Mandela heard about – was the cruellest punishment inflicted on Mandela by the authorities. "Nothing", he wrote later, "tested my inner equilibrium as much as the time that Winnie was in solitary confinement."

During the late 1960s both Mandela's mother and his eldest son died. Mandela was refused permission to attend either funeral.

It is one of the great paradoxes of history that all the isolation, the mental and physical torture, and the hard labour seemed only to strengthen Mandela and his comrades. Robben Island became the university of the new South Africa, where hundreds of prisoners discussed ideas, educated and supported each other, took degrees by correspondence and prepared themselves for the day they would be free, and able to release the country from the tyranny of apartheid. With his colleagues, Mandela had the time – 10 000 days in prison – to contemplate the deepest questions of life, and to find their deepest purpose on this earth. Mandela recalled:

> "I seem to arrive more firmly at the conclusion that my own life struggle has had meaning only because, dimly and perhaps incoherently, it has sought to achieve the supreme objective of ensuring that each, without regard to race, colour, gender and social status, could have the possibility to reach for the skies." ◉◉

Marco de Angelis, 1970

Between 1964 and 1976 the apartheid government had comprehensively bottled up black opposition. Political activity inside the country became almost non-existent in the face of intense repression. Foreign investment poured in and the economy boomed.

"I think I can say without fear of contradiction..."

David Marais, 1970

After the assassination of Hendrik Verwoerd in 1966, Justice Minister John Vorster took over as Prime Minister. Vorster had already established a reputation as the "hard man" of apartheid. Under his prime ministership, which lasted until 1978, the South African Police would be transformed into an effective and deadly repressive force.

Richard Smith & Abbott, 1973

By the late 1960s, the student movements, including the National Union of South African Students (NUSAS) and the Steve Biko-led South African Students Organisation (SASO) were the only significant legal opposition to the government. This wry Smith & Abbott strip does not overstate the risks that student leaders, black and white, took in opposing apartheid. Banning orders became a favourite weapon of the government – such orders confined students to their magisterial districts, subjected them to curfews, and forbade them to meet more than one person at a time.

Clay Bennett, 1985

The ANC in exile had begun reorganising and regrouping in the 1960s. By the early 1970s it had started to win significant victories in mobilising world opinion against the apartheid government. The ANC strategy was to isolate apartheid, building on the victories of South Africa's expulsion from the Commonwealth in 1960, and its exclusion from the Olympics in 1964 and 1970. By the early 1970s limited economic boycotts began to be implemented. This sanctions strategy would become much more effective after the 1976 uprising.

Jimmy Margulies, 1986

By the early 1980s many of the world's largest companies had either chosen or been forced to divest from South Africa. Companies like Pepsi-Cola, Apple computers and Kodak all took the moral high ground by refusing to support the apartheid government. An interesting spin-off around the campaign to isolate South Africa economically was that it transformed debates about business ethics around the world.

Richard Smith, 1973

South Africans, black and white, have always been a sports-mad nation. Some commentators have argued that the sports boycotts, particularly those affecting rugby and cricket, were a key factor in making the white ruling class in South Africa feel their isolation very personally from the rest of the world. This cartoon strip refers to some of the attempts by the South African regime to dress up apartheid as a respectable system of government. Of the many Orwellian terms that the state devised from the 1970s onwards to re-describe apartheid, "vertical differentiation" was the most obtuse.

Rico, 1990

The international cultural boycott of South Africa also started to bite in the 1970s. By the 1980s the only artists who would tour South Africa were either relatively obscure or in the twilight of their careers. The SABC and other government propaganda organs would hype up each visit of a celebrity in an attempt to reassure white South Africans that they were not as isolated as they seemed to be. Most audiences for cultural events, including theatre, musical performances and movies, were segregated until the mid-1980s.

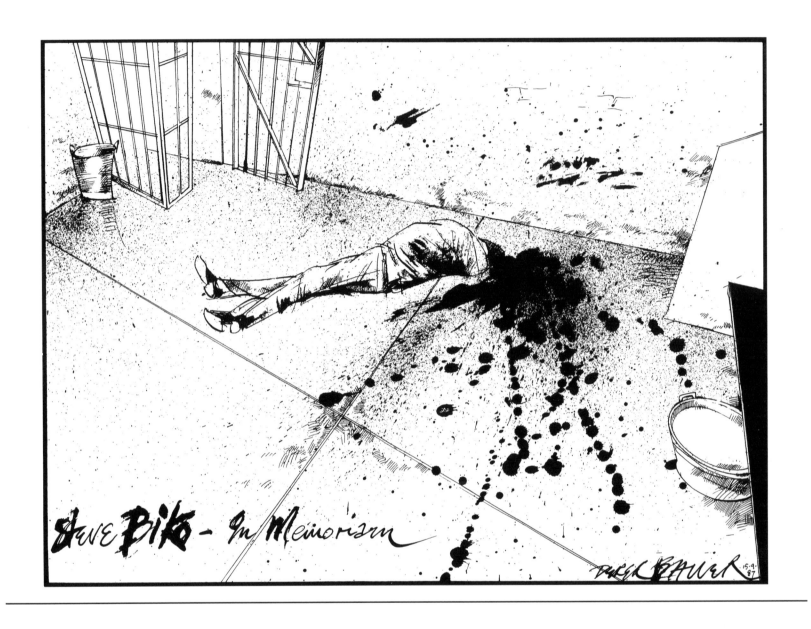

Steve Biko – In Memoriam

Derek Bauer, 1987

In South Africa's schools and universities, the ideas of black consciousness became a powerful organising ideology. Steve Biko, widely regarded as the most impressive leader of his generation, inspired black South Africans to reject the colonial mentality that made blacks see themselves as inferior to whites. This made Biko an extremely dangerous opponent for the apartheid government. In the wake of the 1976 uprisings, a massive clamp-down on political activists was authorised. Tens of thousands of activists were detained, and the phenomena of deaths in detention began occurring with alarming frequency. In September 1977 Steve Biko was detained by the Port Elizabeth security police and severely tortured. Unconscious, he was transferred in the back of a police van to Pretoria, where he died from his injuries.

Chuck Ayers, 1984

In 1984 Bishop Desmond Tutu was awarded the Nobel Peace Prize. The news was announced amid a wave of unprecedented repression that would foreshadow the declaring of a state of emergency. This great honour for Tutu was a clear signal from the world to the apartheid government, and a vindication of Tutu's consistent and vigorous opposition to apartheid.

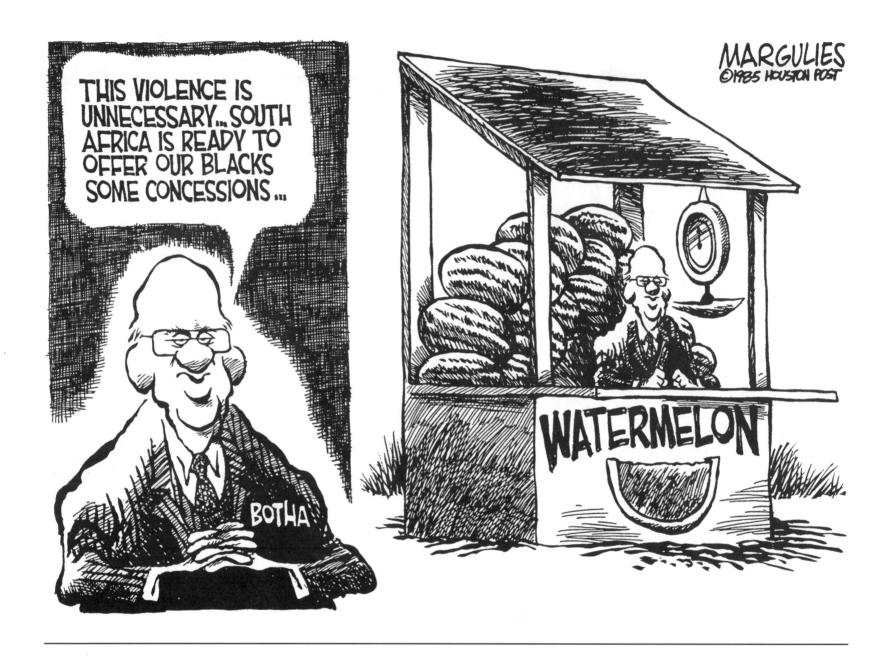

Jimmy Margulies, 1985

Margulies' wry look at the limited concessions that the new Botha government promised black South Africans puns on the American notion of a "concession" store. In American racial politics, the watermelon is the symbol of a stereotypical and crude view of African Americans and their lifestyle.

Steve Bell, 1984

The uprising of 1976 created a deep crisis for the ruling National Party. It had become clear that the hard-line approach of the Vorster era was unsustainable. Reform-minded cabinet minister P.W. Botha engineered a palace coup and became Prime Minister in 1978. Botha styled himself as a radical reformer and set about trying to devise a system which would diffuse black political aspirations and ensure the long-term survival of white political power. Steve Bell's cartoon from this era depicts the hearty support that the British Prime Minister Margaret Thatcher gave the Botha government.

Richard Smith & Abbott, 1973

These two strips by Smith & Abbott depict how bureaucratic and oppressive South Africa's control over the black population was becoming by the mid 1970s. Every black South African was required by law to carry a pass book as well as a variety of other documentation on their person at all times. It was a criminal offence not to be in possession of a pass.

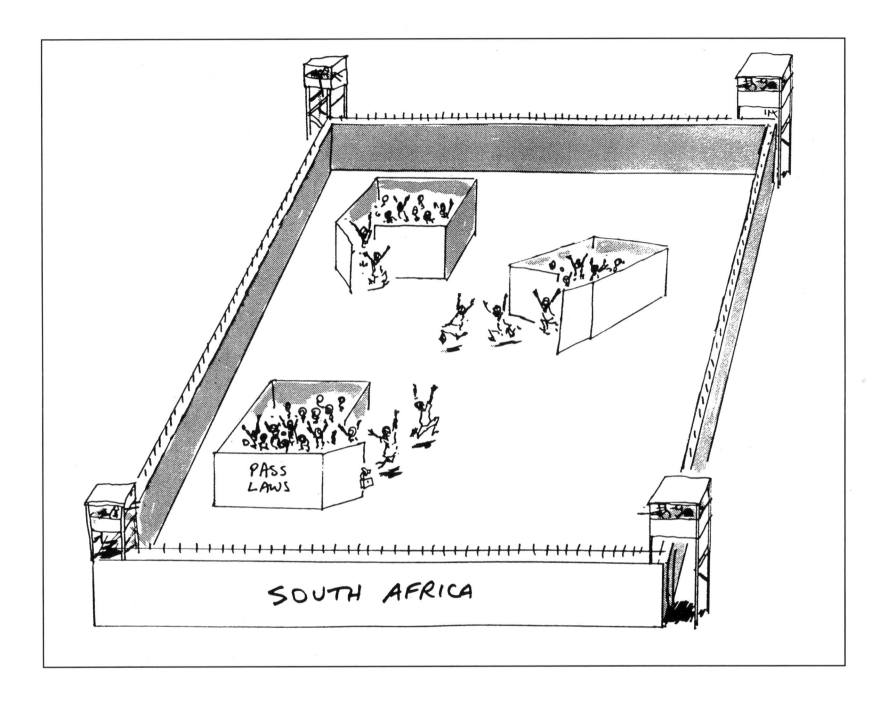

Moir, 1985

Even something as dramatic as repealing the pass laws in 1986 failed to impress the world. The pass laws, also known as influx control regulations, confined black people to particular areas. No black person could be in a designated white area for more than 72 hours, and then only for the purposes of looking for work. At the height of apartheid, the South African Police arrested more than a million black South Africans per year for pass law violations.

Jules Feiffer, 1984

The tortured logic by which right-wing Republicans in the United States justified support for the apartheid government is perfectly summarised by Jules Feiffer's satirical depiction of a conversation between right-wing preacher Jerry Falwell and American President Ronald Reagan.

"REMEMBER—NO MATTER HOW IT LOOKS, I'M ON YOUR SIDE!"

Marlette, 1987

South Africa produced almost half the world's gold, more than half of its diamonds and very substantial amounts of crucial strategic minerals like platinum and cobalt. The US was determined to do nothing which would undermine the West's access to these minerals. There is evidence that the CIA collaborated with the security police in South Africa to help keep a lid on the opposition. A long-standing allegation even suggests that a CIA tip-off led to Mandela's arrest at a roadblock in 1962.

Derek Bauer, 1980

The government of P.W. Botha steadfastly refused to talk with any genuine black leaders. They insisted on speaking only to "moderate" leaders – which basically meant black leaders who supported the apartheid system. By 1980 Derek Bauer was gaining a formidable reputation for his uncompromising cartoons; this seering image would enhance that reputation.

Auth, 1986

By the early 1980s, South Africa was ostracised throughout the world. As the Botha government intensified its repression, the ANC made an all-out push for economic sanctions. Most democratic countries in the world imposed sanctions of some kind, but the UK and the USA were extremely reluctant to do so. They argued that the Botha government was open to moral argument, and could be convinced to voluntarily abandon apartheid through a process of dialogue which they called "constructive engagement". As recently as the late 1980s Margaret Thatcher referred to Mandela as a "terrorist" and said that anyone who thought the ANC would ever rule in South Africa was "living in cloud cuckooland".

Derek Bauer, 1987

Throughout the Botha era, South Africa continued with the fiction that it held no political prisoners – only ordinary convicted criminals who didn't deserve any kind of special treatment. In fact, political prisoners such as Mandela were often treated less well than ordinary criminal prisoners. By the 1980s torture was routine, as were lengthy spells of solitary confinement before trial. By the time political prisoners were sentenced, they had usually undergone severe ordeals, and their families continued to attract the special treatment of the security forces long after the prisoners were sentenced.

Len Sak, 1987

By the early 1980s, Nelson Mandela had become a symbol of world resistance to apartheid. Hundreds of streets, public squares and parks, students' unions and community facilities were named in Mandela's honour. A concert held to celebrate his 70th birthday, by which time he had been in jail for 23 years, attracted more than 250 000 people to London's Hyde Park.

"SOME DAY, SON, THIS WILL ALL BE YOURS..."

Auth, 1985

The ANC, supported by internal resistance movements like the United Democratic Front (UDF), took an active decision to make South Africa ungovernable. By 1985 the situation inside the country had reached crisis point with uprisings, strikes, boycotts and armed resistance reaching unprecedented levels.

Chapter 3

State of emergency

Paul Fell

By 1985 South Africa was in a deep crisis, unprecedented even in its long and tragic history. A civil war had broken out and the relative calm produced by intense repression that had prevailed up to 1976 and again, briefly, from 1978 to 1981 was over. Mandela and other political leaders had been in prison for 21 years and the ANC and PAC had been banned for 25 years. Thousands of political activists had been killed, the number of deaths in detention had exceeded a hundred, and many activists were banned and placed under house arrest. Despite building the biggest army in Africa, the government's "total strategy" to meet what it described as the ANC-led "total onslaught" was losing ground to the forces of change. The ANC's call in the mid-1980s to make the country "ungovernable" was beginning to take effect.

TRYING TRICAMERAL

For almost a decade the National Party had been manoeuvring through a complex strategy of divide, conquer and rule, giving small concessions with the one hand, and clamping down on any opposition with the other. In response to the uprising of 1976, and South Africa's growing isolation from the rest of the world, the National Party elected a new Prime Minister in 1978 – the hard-line former Minister of Defence, P.W. Botha. Botha championed what the Nationalists touted as a big

new idea – the introduction of a complex new constitution with the fairly obvious aim of further dividing black opposition. This new reform package, heralded with much triumph, had three interlocking parts:

- to partly enfranchise coloured and Indian South Africans, and create three separate parliaments for whites, coloured and Indians which would be called the "tricameral" parliament
- to accelerate the creation of independent homelands for Africans, and give them wider powers
- to recognise the reality of the urban African population by dropping the pass laws, and allowing urban Africans to vote for the first time, but only for their local town councils – lifeless bodies with almost no real powers.

The idea was to win support for apartheid from the coloured and Indian middle class, who could then shore up the system together with the white population. Plans to conscript coloured and Indian males into the apartheid army were to follow the elections due to be held in 1983. The government still clung tenaciously to the homeland system as providing the primary political home for Africans, and hoped that the new vote for local town councils would satisfy black political aspirations in the urban areas.

HOUSES DIVIDED

But these grand reforms started going wrong almost as soon as they were implemented. The coloureds and Indians whom Botha hoped to co-opt into the system were equally disgusted with the proposed "tricameral parliament" – three separate houses, one for each ethnic group, divided along racial lines, with the white parliament having a veto over all decisions. The few coloured and Indian politicians who could be enticed by promises of personal reward into standing for the new chambers became a national joke when voters responded favourably to a UDF led boycott, and stayed away from the elections in droves. About 30% of coloureds voted, as did 10% of Indians. One Indian MP entered the record books – and the Indian chamber – with a 0.01% poll – even his own family had not voted for him and he had neglected to vote for himself!

TAKING THE GAP

But the reforms and tricameral elections also provided new opportunities for opposition groupings. To give a veneer of respectability to the elections, the government had to allow the expression of real opposition. Organisations like the newly formed United Democratic Front (UDF), a movement with direct links to the ANC, actively called for a boycott of the elections. This sudden space to organise was unprecedented since the 1950s, and opposition groups seized upon it with enthusiasm.

After the elections took place, South Africa began to resemble a war zone. The government took the gloves off, furious at the way the UDF and the Congress of South African Trade Unions (COSATU) had disrupted and discredited the tricameral parliament. 1984 was a hellish year for South Africa – Orwellian in its outright repression, encouraging a depth of resistance that was growing inside the country and internationally. It seemed that in every village and small town, a broadly ANC-supporting youth congress or women's movement was taking root. The government was also steadily losing control of the urban black areas.

In March 1985 the army was mobilised to help put down the rapidly escalating protests that rocked many of the black townships. At Langa township near Uitenhage soldiers shot at unarmed men, women and children who were marching to attend a funeral. Twenty people were killed. In response, Langa residents went on the rampage, killing, among others, the last remaining town councillor in KwaNobuhle township.

In the face of sustained insurrection, P.W. Botha ordered a crackdown, announcing the declaration of a state of emergency on 20 July in certain parts of the country. The security forces were given even wider powers to detain without trial, to ban newspapers, prohibit gatherings (including funerals) and to impose a complete press gag on the coverage of all "unrest" activities and police actions.

CROSSING THE RUBICON

The world expressed strong disapproval of the state of emergency and warned of heavy economic sanctions. To assuage the international community, the Nationalists gave strong hints that dramatic reforms would be announced in a major speech which Botha would give in August 1985. International interest was intense, particularly in the United States and Britain where Reagan and Thatcher had held back sanctions by promising that significant changes were imminent. P.W. Botha's speech started promisingly with the phrase that South Africa had "crossed the Rubicon", a reference to Julius Caesar's irrevocable crossing of that famous river in 49 BC. But then Botha lost the plot and the speech disintegrated into a wild condemnation of the West and a promise to crack down hard on dissent within South Africa. Botha effectively told the West, including his few remaining friends, Reagan and Thatcher, to "go to hell". Later he said South Africa would not "crawl" to avoid sanctions and would go it alone if necessary.

Botha withdrew further into his State Security Council, a body that began to supersede ordinary cabinet meetings. Even National Party ministers began to talk about the "Imperial Presidency". Inside the country the crisis was still deteriorating, despite more than 20 000 arrests.

PEOPLE'S POWER

International response to the infamous "Rubicon speech" was swift – even the US Congress passed a "comprehensive" anti-apartheid sanctions bill, which forbade the importation of South African iron, oil, coal and several other categories of goods. Scores of companies divested from South Africa. For the British government, Thatcher's hard-line support for the National Party was becoming a serious embarrassment.

In the first three months of the state of emergency at least 500 people in South Africa had been killed by police gunfire, more than 20 000 people had been injured, 14 000 arrests had been made and 5000 people had been detained without trial. The low-intensity civil war of the past was being replaced with a hardening of attitudes and tactics. The ANC controversially revealed that the line between "soft" (civilian) and "hard" (military) targets would start to blur. Whole sections of South Africa were transformed into no-go areas for troops and police, as black communities organised themselves into People's Committees. These informal structures developed to such an extent in some areas that they administered townships as "liberated zones", building up alternative structures to carry out even mundane civic duties such as collecting rubbish and staffing clinics. These committees gave substance to the call for "People's Power". The structures which emerged on the ground, from "district" to "street" committees, bore a strong resemblance to Mandela's "M Plan", advocated for the underground organisation of the ANC during the late 1950s and early 1960s. Arms caches were established in some areas and trained ANC guerrillas were hidden and protected by local communities.

TALKING TO THE "TERRORIST"

In April 1986 Botha made the hollow claim that conditions had returned to "normal" and lifted the state of emergency. By this time 3500 houses had been destroyed, 1220 schools burnt to the ground, 7000 buses were damaged. The "Rubicon" speech had caused such political and economic damage (a panic run on the South African currency had caused it to plummet from 52 to 33 US cents) that Botha was growing desperate for a way out, even considering talking directly to Nelson Mandela. Mandela had been moved from Robben Island to Victor Verster Prison and placed in a house in the grounds to facilitate talks. Minister of Justice Kobie Coetsee had already met the famous prisoner several times.

In order to have sanctions eased Botha wanted to show the international community that he was flexible, but he argued that he himself could not talk directly with a "terrorist", as he called Mandela, lest this lead to further losses to the Conservative Party, which had formed to the right of his National Party. He offered Mandela his freedom provided Mandela renounced violence. Mandela's response was swift "Let Botha renounce violence. Let him say that he will dismantle Apartheid." Sadly there was little chance of this happening.

Violence soon broke out again, particularly in the form of the gruesome "necklacing" in black townships. Black policemen, town councillors and informers became particular targets for this grisly method of execution. Winnie Mandela's announcement exemplified these volatile and violent times: "the time for speeches and debate has come to an end... together, hand in hand with our sticks and our matches, with our necklaces, we shall liberate this country."

EMINENT PERSONS

An attempt to resolve the crisis now came from outside South Africa. A respected group of statesmen from the Commonwealth of Nations, the Eminent Persons Group

(EPG), visited Mandela in prison and tried to persuade Botha to start serious negotiations on South Africa's future. However, just as with the Rubicon speech, Botha lacked the courage to do so. He was under heavy pressure from security forces in his Security Council and gave in to the "hawks" led by Defence Minister Magnus Malan. On the morning of 19 May, the same day that the EPG was to visit the cabinet, Botha permitted Malan to launch a dramatic air strike against alleged ANC bases in Zambia, Zimbabwe and Botswana. On 12 June, Botha declared a second, nation-wide state of emergency, far more stringent and draconian than its predecessor. In the words of US diplomat Chester Crocker, "something snapped in the man".

For the next two years the country was plunged into a sustained recession, comprehensive news blackouts, mass detentions, the banning of the UDF, even the jailing of white conscientious objectors who refused to serve in the apartheid army in the townships. A black worker was sentenced to a substantial prison term for carving the letters "ANC" on to his tea mug. Government hit squads started to operate with great impunity. ANC sabotage attacks became increasingly deadly and frequent.

Mandela, having been transferred from Robben Island to Pollsmoor Prison, and then to Victor Verster, was heartened by the mass uprisings and the militancy of the struggle against the government. He had responded eloquently to the 1988 offer of release, and his speech was read out to a political rally in Soweto by his daughter Zindzi, to great acclaim. His famous speech included the words:

"I cherish my own freedom dearly, but I care even more for your freedom. Too many have died since I went to prison. Too many have suffered for the love of freedom. I owe it to their widows, to their orphans, to their mothers and to their fathers who have grieved and wept for them. Not only I have suffered during these long, lonely, wasted years. I am no less life-loving than you are. But I cannot sell my birthright, nor am I prepared to sell the birthright of the people, to be free. Only free men can negotiate. Prisoners cannot enter into contracts. I cannot and will not give any undertaking at a time when I and you, the people, are not free. Your freedom and mine cannot be separated. I will return." ◉◉

The famous French cartoonist, Plantu's, take on the Eminent Persons' last-ditch attempt to facilitate negotiations in South Africa. The S.A. government is telling the human rights campaigner, "But he fired first."

Plantu

Jimmy Margulies, 1985

By the mid-1980s there was a strong sense that the apartheid government was running out of time. But even at the height of the crisis in 1985, when, for the first time, the ability of the government to hold it all together came under serious question, very few people would have predicted that the apartheid regime would survive only another five years. It would be fair to say that even the most optimistic activists believed that ten to fifteen years of increasingly violent low-intensity civil war lay ahead for South Africa.

Scrawls, 1985

By 1985 P.W. Botha's government had given up all pretence of being able to manage the growing crisis in the country through any means other than open repression. For a reformer who had said many times that repression could only be a short-term solution, and that winning black "hearts and minds" was the key to long-term stability, P.W. Botha knew that his state of emergency would bring only temporary respite.

Auth, 1985

The state of emergency brought with it even more draconian anti-press legislation than ever before. The South African government argued that the otherwise "peaceful" black population was incited to riot by the presence of press cameras. Many parts of South Africa were declared "no-go" areas for the press, and scores of journalists were detained.

Shakespere, 1985

The argument that the presence of cameras caused riots was of course nonsense. Video footage of police and army brutality had become one of the most powerful factors in convincing the world that ever-harsher means were necessary to defeat the apartheid government. The police were determined to keep this torrid footage out of the world's gaze.

Raeside, 1985

South Africa became a hazardous place for journalists, particularly
black journalists, many of whom were detained without trial for
long periods in the mid-1980s.

Stent, 1989

White South Africans were never monolithically in favour of apartheid. In the 1960s and 1970s support for the ANC came mostly from the white liberal campuses, and in particular from the National Union of South African Students (NUSAS). In the 1980s, organisations like the End Conscription Campaign (ECC) challenged a younger generation of young white South Africans to oppose apartheid. Political T-shirts became collectors items.

Richard Smith, 1984

From the early 1980s, South African security forces decided to strike at the ANC throughout Africa. Numerous "cross-border raids" were authorised and South African jet fighters and commandos inflicted heavy casualties in Zimbabwe, Zambia, Mozambique and other "front-line" states.

Zapiro, 1987

The security forces also sought to exacerbate tensions between liberation movements in South Africa, and to pin the blame for many of the worst security-force massacres on "black on black violence". This divide-and-rule strategy was employed with particular effect in the Eastern Cape, Natal and townships around Johannesburg, including Soweto. Black *agents provocateurs* were also deployed with greater effectiveness from the early 1980s onwards.

Zapiro, 1987

With the declaration of the state of emergency, South African police and army units began attacking alleged ANC operations with renewed vigour. International borders provided little obstacle to the SADF's attacks. Zambia was particularly hard hit as the ANC headquarters were based in Lusaka for much of the 1970s and 1980s.

"YOUR CHILD WAS KILLED AT MY CHILD'S FUNERAL?... I THOUGHT MY CHILD WAS KILLED AT YOUR CHILD'S FUNERAL!"

Marlette, 1985

This poignant and grim cartoon bears witness to the terrible spiral of resistance and intensified repression that characterised the last five years of apartheid rule. With almost every form of political protest outlawed (including marches, demonstrations, pickets and mass organisations), funerals became a key method of mobilising resistance. Funerals often attracted hundreds of thousands of mourners and, almost inevitably, some would be killed by the security forces. This would lead to yet another funeral/mass rally the next weekend.

Zapiro, 1987

Zapiro's wonderful parody of the fairy tale "The Emperor's New Clothes" sees President P.W. Botha sending his namesake, Stoffel Botha, to attack the flourishing alternative press. Stoffel Botha, in charge of the absurdly named Ministry of Information, was the scourge of journalists trying to tell the truth about what was happening in South Africa. The South African Broadcasting Corporation (SABC), the only broadcaster allowed to transmit the news on radio or television, never failed to provide the government's view on the deteriorating South African situation.

LISTEN MANDELA – I'M THE ONE WHO CALLS THE SHOTS AROUND HERE!

Ken, 1983

This cartoon, one of the very first to refer to Nelson Mandela, appeared in the UK in 1983. Mandela's profile both inside and outside of the country grew in leaps and bounds in the first few years of the 1980s.

Zapiro, 1987

In 1987 the apartheid government commemorated the 75th anniversary of the South African Defence Force. Here, P.W. Botha is depicted celebrating with his three top securocrats: Minister of Police Adriaan Vlok, Chief of the Defence Force, Jannie Geldenhuys, and Defence Minister Magnus Malan.

The ANC, represented in this cartoon by its President, Oliver Tambo, was also celebrating its 75th anniversary, and was enjoying a surge in international and local support. The Afrikaans phrase "Blerrie snaaks" means "Bloody funny", or words to that effect.

Ken, 1983

By the 1980s, Mandela had been transformed from a relatively obscure political prisoner in South Africa, to a world-renowned icon. In the UK and in much of Europe, the movement to free Mandela and other South African political prisoners gathered momentum from about 1981.

Mynderd Vosloo, 1985

Even after the imposition of the state of emergency, the white government was determined to get some form of negotiation going with black leaders over what it called "power-sharing". No one was entirely clear about what power would be shared with whom, and finding credible blacks to talk to proved impossible. It was at this stage that the government of P.W. Botha, depicted here as a firefighter, first started exploring the possibility of talking to the ANC.

Zapiro, 1985

Despite the crisis, or perhaps because of it, P.W. Botha's calls for black negotiating partners became more strident. But the National Party now made a song and dance about what it thought was an eminently reasonable new precondition: that the black leaders would no longer have to be "moderate" but would have to "renounce violence" before negotiations could begin.

MR MANDELA'S GOODWILL VISIT TO THE STATE PRESIDENT.

Andy, 1986

For Mandela the process of negotiating secretly with the government, which had totally isolated him from the rest of the ANC leadership, was fraught with danger. As he notes in his autobiography, *Long Walk to Freedom*: "I was not happy to be separated from my colleagues, and I missed my garden and sunny terrace. But my solitude gave me a certain liberty and I resolved to use it to do something I had been pondering for a long while: begin discussions with the government."

A STEP CLOSER ?

Andy, 1986

In 1985 P.W. Botha had initiated the transfer of Nelson Mandela from Robben Island to Pollsmoor Prison, and later to Victor Verster Prison. The crocodile that Mandela seems about to step on can be construed as a reference to Botha, who was unaffectionately known as the "Groot Krokodil" (the Big Crocodile).

It was at Victor Verster that Mandela took the leap of faith that changed the history of South Africa. As he recalls in his autobiography, "I chose to tell no one what I was about to do... I did not have the security at the time to discuss the issues with my organisation. I knew that my collegues upstairs would condemn my proposal, and that would kill my initiative even before it was born." This was one of Mandela's bravest actions in a long history of courageous decisions.

Marlene Moultrie, 1986

Mandela refused to negotiate with the government on its terms. In his famous smuggled speech of February 1985, the first time Mandela's words had been heard in public since 1964, Mandela challenged P.W. Botha directly: "What freedom am I being offered when my very South African citizenship is not respected? Only free men can negotiate. Prisoners cannot enter into contracts."

Grogan, 1985

Grogan's deceptively simple cartoon captures the stalemate of the 1985 talks-about-talks perfectly. Mandela was typically sanguine about his decision to ultimately begin talks with the government. He knew his isolation would provide the ANC with an excuse if the negotiations went wrong – and he was prepared to be the scapegoat. He remembered, "My isolation furnished my organisation with an excuse in case matters went awry: the old man was alone and completely cut off, and his actions were taken by him as an individual and not as a representative of the ANC."

Zapiro, 1987

Despite ongoing secret negotiation, an ever more desperate apartheid government needed a face-saving way to release Mandela and other political prisoners. Botha, above anyone else, was determined not to be seen as "soft". In 1987 he started suggesting bizarre prison swap arrangements in order to find a politically acceptable way of releasing Mandela. At one stage Botha wanted to offer Mandela's release for the release of a captured South African soldier, Captain Du Toit, together with Andrei Sakharov, a Russian dissident. The world was decidedly unimpressed.

"DON'T THESE IDIOTS KNOW THAT HE COULD BE AS FREE AS GOVAN MBEKI?"

Andy, 1988

In 1988 ANC stalwart Govan Mbeki, father of Mandela's successor as President, Thabo Mbeki, was released from jail, and immediately placed under a restriction order.

The government was testing the waters by releasing a high-profile leader, but still lacked the courage to do it without restrictions.

Derek Bauer, 1989

This famous cartoon by Derek Bauer captures the arrogance of the National Party government and of P.W. Botha in particular. With crippling international sanctions in place and internal resistance increasing in intensity, the writing was on the wall for the apartheid government by 1989.

Chapter 4

Free at last

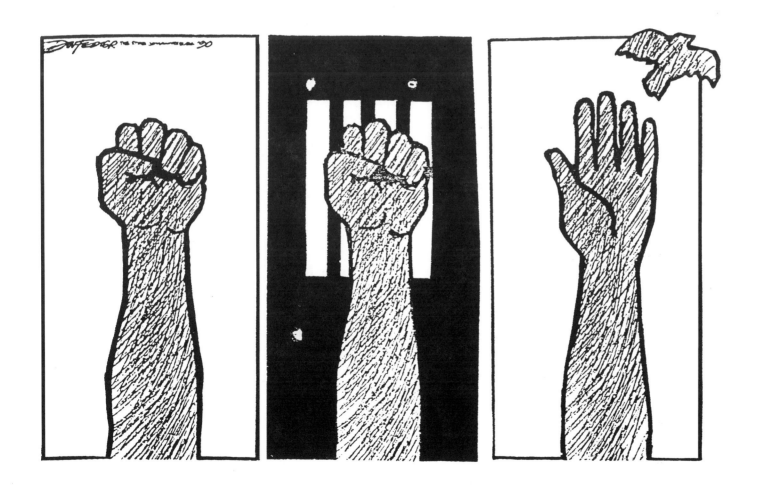

Dov Fedler

P.W. Botha suffered a stroke on 18 January 1989. A little over two years later, Nelson Mandela was walking free and the ANC was unbanned.

In-between these two events lay a thousand incremental steps. In the wake of P.W.'s stroke, a relatively obscure National Party cabinet minister, F.W. de Klerk, came to power. He would play a crucial role in bringing change to South Africa in an astonishingly short time. De Klerk had a reputation as a *verkrampte* (conservative) and had notoriously failed to support Botha's scrapping of petty apartheid in 1985. He was chosen as the head of the party in the Transvaal partly because his conservatism was seen as the only way to keep the party in line in a province where the Conservative Party was making in-roads. His ministerial control over education was not marked by any reforms. He was also not part of P.W.'s inner circle and later greatly resented the exclusion, particularly since he had not been told about the secret talks that had been going on with Mandela since 1985.

Though no longer the head of the party, P.W. Botha retained his position as State President after his stroke. This created a constitutional crisis for the Nationalists, as the head of the party had always been the head of government. After several months of increasing tensions, the "clash of the bald eagles", as a weekly newspaper described it, came to a head when P.W. was called to a cabinet meeting on 10 August 1989. Botha was encouraged by his colleagues to go gracefully. He refused, only to resign noisily on national television that night.

WHAT MADE DE KLERK CHANGE HIS MIND?

The country was in turmoil. The ANC was at the height of its powers, making inroads in every part of the country, fêted abroad, striking hard at high-profile government targets, including South Africa's first nuclear power plant. But De Klerk had the resources, a ruthless security apparatus and the best-equipped army in Africa. He could have held on, probably for another decade.

De Klerk has long denied that he had a "road to Damascus" experience that caused him to review his own beliefs or that of his party. But there is evidence that De Klerk, a religious man felt a "calling" to "save" South Africa, and that he had been deeply moved by his inauguration sermon in which he was warned by the minister from his own church that South Africa was stuck in a "groove" that could lead to a "grave".
De Klerk's pragmatism also enabled him to see that sanctions were beginning to exact a heavy toll and that black protests would not go away but would rather grow more strident and effective. Probably one of the most profound influences on his decision was the collapse of socialism in Eastern Europe and the implosion of the Soviet Union itself in 1989 and 1990. In one stroke, the *rooi gevaar* ("red danger") was removed and it became easier to speak to African "nationalists" rather than the "communist" dominated ANC.

DIVIDE AND RULE

De Klerk was also a hardened and wily politician. As a lawyer he had a famous sense of timing, which he brought into his political life. He reasoned, along with his cabinet, that if the

Nationalists made a number of far-reaching reforms, and did so quickly, this would "unbalance" their enemies at home and abroad. In this way the Nationalists, by garnering the goodwill that such reforms would produce, could manoeuvre themselves into a position where it was even possible they could emerge as a winning party in any democratic elections. De Klerk, in any case, felt that in a system of "power-sharing", with a bill of rights and a constitution that required different parties to reach consensus before passing new laws, it would be possible for whites or Afrikaners to hold on to power as a "group" protecting its "group rights".

In short, F.W. believed that he could outwit the opposition. Only later did it become clear that his strategy also included unleashing a secret war on the ANC and its supporters.

On 2 February 1990, De Klerk made a dramatic speech to parliament. He unbanned the African National Congress, the South African Communist Party and the Pan Africanist Congress and declared his willingness to negotiate on South Africa's future with these parties. Although the Conservative Party noisily walked out of parliament calling F.W. a *volksveraaier* (a traitor, betraying his people), the rest of the country was first stunned and then elated.

FREE AT LAST

Then the miracle happened. On 11 February 1990, Nelson Mandela walked out of prison as a free man. In much the same way that Americans still remember vividly the assassination of President J.F. Kennedy, or the sight of American astronaut Neil Armstrong walking on the moon, the image of Mandela stepping to freedom with Winnie Mandela by his side was burnt into the consciousness of South Africans. Walking stiffly but with great dignity, Mandela could not help himself: he broke out in a huge grin and waved enthusiastically at the ecstatic crowd. It was a moment unequalled in South African history.

As Mandela recalled in his autobiography:
"At first I could not really make out what was going on, but when I was within 150 feet or so, I saw a great crowd of people; hundreds of photographers and television cameras and newspeople as well as several thousand well-wishers. I was astounded and a little alarmed. When I was among the crowd I raised my right fist, and there was a roar. I had not been able to do that for twenty-seven years and it gave me a surge of strength and joy. As I finally walked through those gates I felt – even at the age of seventy-one – that my life was beginning anew. My ten thousand days of imprisonment were at last over." ൭

Auth

Tinus Horn, 1990

F.W. de Klerk decided to go for broke – unban all politicial organisations including the ANC and begin a process of negotiation around power-sharing. The National Party was confident that it could string out the negotiations for years to come, possibly even for a decade or so, and that in the process it could weaken the ANC substantially. In this cartoon De Klerk is saying, "We free him, we don't free him, we free him, we don't free him, we free him, we don't free him."

Lynch, 1989

A common theme of cartoons in late 1989 was Mandela's imminent release and his legendary near-mythical status. At this point, no one outside of apartheid jails knew what Nelson Mandela looked like.

Pugh, 1991

This Pugh cartoon from the British satirical magazine *Private Eye*
poignantly captures the importance of Nelson Mandela to the
entire world.

Miel, 1990

Nelson Mandela was released from prison on 11 February 1990.

He had been in jail for a little over 27 years.

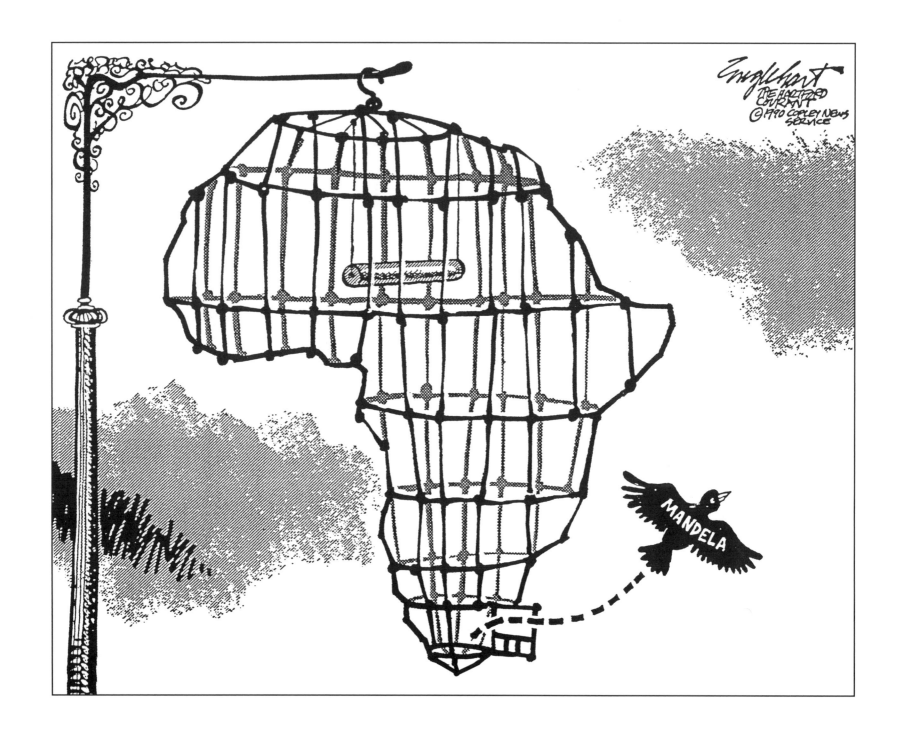

Engelhart, 1990

The whole of Africa welcomed Mandela's release as if a new spirit
of freedom had been released upon the continent.

Chapter 5

Negotiations and transitions

Derek Bauer

In the early months after his release, both Mandela and De Klerk enjoyed a "honeymoon" period despite the many frustrations and disappointments that came their way. In his famous speech to an adoring Cape Town crowd on the day of his freedom, Mandela called De Klerk a "man of integrity" who had gone further than any of his predecessors to "normalise the situation" in South Africa. Mandela also warned, however, that the struggle was entering its most crucial phase and that "now is the time to intensify the struggle on all fronts".

As late as December 1990, Mandela confided that he and De Klerk had developed "enormous respect" for one another and would call each other late at night, putting aside everything to talk. Yet violence continued to plague the country, reaching a crisis point when, in the middle of the year, a serious clash between ANC and Inkatha forces leapt like a flame from KwaZulu-Natal to the Witwatersrand's townships, the economic heartland of South Africa. Chief Buthelezi had relaunched his Inkatha movement on 14 July 1990 as a political alternative to the ANC. Zulu-speaking

migrant workers living in the bleak barracks of the hostels in the townships had long felt alienated from the township residents who spoke other languages and who feared the Zulu workers as rough and poorly educated thugs. Just eight days after Inkatha's launch, a clash between their supporters and ANC supporters on the Rand left thirty people dead.

THE THIRD FORCE

The police seemed to do little to stop these attacks. In fact there was mounting evidence that they actively promoted Inkatha attacks on ANC supporters and even took part in them. This began to sour Mandela's impression of De Klerk as there were only two possible explanations for rumours of a "Third Force" of disgruntled security forces behind the violence: either De Klerk had ordered them or else he could not control them. Either of these scenarios was unacceptable to Mandela and he began to lose faith in De Klerk.

Negotiations proceeded at a painfully slow pace. Only by December 1991, after 23 months of "talks-about-talks" did the first serious all-party discussion begin in ernest. These discussions labelled, "The Convention for a Democratic South Africa",

Kambiz Derambahsh

or CODESA, were fraught from the begining, and were interupted by an all-white referendum in March 1992. It would be the last ever whites-only plebiscite – 69% of the white population voted to support the negotiations. While the referendum was taking place it became clear that security forces had been behind at least some of the violence. By 1992 over ten people were being killed a day in the political conflict and Mandela's and the ANC's patience was wearing thin.

Then, on 17 June 1992, 200 Inkatha supporters from KwaMadala hostel in Vanderbijlpark, south of Johannesburg, attacked a "squatter" camp at Boipatong. A total of 46 men, women and children died. Mandela's temper snapped. The people who had been responsible for this "were animals" and in the next breath he said, "We will not forget what Mr de Klerk, the National Party and the Inkatha Freedom Party have done to our people. I have never seen such cruelty." The honeymoon was over; indeed a divorce was in the air. The ANC walked out of the CODESA talks and began a campaign of "rolling mass action". At some marches as many as 200 000 angry protesters took part.

The ANC also took the fight to the "homelands", long a thorn in their side. In Ciskei, a particularly offensive leader, Oupa Gqozo, was chosen as a target for the "Leipzig Option", a strategy of mass upheaval to bring about a tyrant's fall, as had happened with Honecker in East Germany. A march to King William's Town, led by ANC leader Ronnie Kasrils, became a cover for a sudden "run" on Bisho, the nearby capital of Ciskei. The Ciskeian troops opened fire and 28 marchers were killed and over 200 were wounded.

Shaken by the experience, the ANC tried to get negotiations back on track by streamlining their demands, insisting on the banning of "cultural weapons", firm control of hostels at the centre of the violence, and the release of 200 political prisoners. Although De Klerk balked at all three demands, Mandela would not give in: "we hold the line here", he told his negotiating team.

TOUGH AS NAILS

One colleague, Cyril Ramaphosa, later said that Mandela was "as tough as nails". He got what he wanted and by the end of 1992 negotiations resumed. But, as Ramaphosa observed, the balance had altered: Mandela now had the upper hand.

Nonetheless, the agreements were brittle and could not easily survive another Boipatong. On 10 April 1993 an event even more dire occurred. The General Secretary of the SACP, Chris Hani, a popular and charismatic leader, was gunned down in cold blood by ultra-right wingers. At no other point in South Africa's history had the country's fate been so delicately balanced. But Mandela and De Klerk held their nerve and the country pulled through the crisis, which could easily have disintegrated into full-scale civil war. Both men were deeply shaken, realising that a single madman could cause all the patient, hard-won success to crumble before their eyes.

A new sense of purpose filled the hearts and minds of the main negotiating parties, and the talks speeded up dramatically. Not even the desperate action of the neo-fascist AWB in crashing an armoured car into the World Trade Centre on 25 June, and then "occupying" the negotiating forum while harassing the delegates, could weaken their new-found resolve. Agreement was reached and it was decided that on 27 April 1994 South Africa would go to the polls for the first-ever democratic elections. ◉◉

Chip (formerly Don), 1990

The negotiations of 1990 began tentatively. Two meetings were held, the first at the historic official residence of Groote Schuur, and the second in Pretoria. These produced the Groote Schuur and Pretoria Minutes, which outlined the basic conditions for negotiations. The ANC was particularly concerned to ensure that key party members were released from jail and were given amnesty. The National Party wanted the ANC to abandon the armed struggle entirely, which the ANC initially refused to do.

Lou Henning, 1990

The Groote Schuur and Pretoria Minutes provided much opportunity for commentators to pun. This cartoon by Lou Henning is the cleverest, describing as it does Mandela and De Klerk moving the hands of the clock away from the disaster of midnight. The reference is to the nuclear nightmare: for forty years American scientists against nuclear weapons have issued an annual assessment of how far the world is away from nuclear warfare – or how close – use the the minutes to midnight analogy.

Len Sak, 1990

Right from the start of the negotiations the National Party wanted a wide variety of guarantees that would entrench some kind of white minority veto. Other more right-wing Afrikaners insisted on the establishment of a *volkstaat* or white ethnic homeland where Afrikaners would be in the majority. In this cartoon, Mandela points to Robben Island, where he was held prisoner, as the only place where Afrikaners might form a majority. The man he is talking to is Kobie Coetsee, the cabinet minister who had initiated negotiations with Mandela four years prior to his release.

WHILE YOU DO THAT.... WE'LL NEGOTIATE
WITH THE UNDERTAKERS !!

Nanda Soobben, 1990

Within days of announcing the decision to start negotiating with the ANC on 2 February 1990, violence mysteriously broke out in many areas of the country. This would in fact become a common pattern for the next three years – whenever progress had been made in negotiations, sinister and then unknown "third force elements" would massacre innocent civilians. Later it would be revealed that this was part of a broader government strategy to drag out the negotiations and weaken support for the ANC.

Derek Bauer, 1991

Mandela made numerous attempts to meet with the leader of the IFP, Chief Buthelezi, to discuss the violence in the country but this had no effect in stemming the violence, for which Buthelezi denied responsibility. In later years, Buthelezi and the National Party government would be severely embarrassed by revelations of security force funding and arming of Inkatha death squads.

Stidy, 1997

In 1993 and 1994 the IFP unleashed waves of violence across the country. Chief Buthelezi also proved to be the most intractable negotiator, boycotting the entire CODESA talks, as well as those leading up to the elections of 1994. Buthelezi even refused to participate in the elections itself until eight days before they were due to be held. After the election, the ANC-led government tried everything to mollify Chief Buthelezi and co-opt him into the reconstruction of South Africa. He was made Deputy President, and on numerous occasions when both Mandela and Thabo Mbeki were out of South Africa, Buthelezi acted as President of the country. As distasteful as this attempt to accommodate Buthelezi might seem, it did finally bring peace to KwaZulu-Natal.

Len Sak, 1991

F.W. de Klerk needed to reassure his largely white constituency that negotiations were the only way forward. The government did a fairly good job in this regard. Despite losing badly in some rural by-elections, almost 70% of whites voted in favour of continung negotiations with the ANC in March 1992.

Dov Fedler, 1990

In a merciless attempt to discredit the negotiation process and the ANC, the security forces unleashed wave after wave of train massacres. From 1990 to 1992, travelling on a train – as millions of black South Africans were forced to do because of the long distances imposed by apartheid between home and work – became extremely hazardous. Balaclava'd men would walk through compartments shooting people at random. This would occur routinely after any kind of progress was made in the negotiations.

Len Sak, 1991

The negotiations went very slowly to the ANC's intense frustration. The ANC resorted to playing its strongest card – mobilising the mass of its supporters in demonstrations, marches and strikes, to pressurise the National Party to make concessions.

Chip (formerly Don), 1992

In 1992, after the terrible massacre at Boipatong, Mandela led the ANC out of the negotiations with the government. Mandela was furious with De Klerk, pointing out how the feared security police, who had once been so effective in detaining the ANC leadership, was suddenly unable to stop the violence against the civilian black population. Mandela suspected, rightly as it turns out, that the government either was behind the violence or at least condoned it as a counter negotiating tactic. Mandela set 14 conditions for the resumption of talks, many of which had to do with more effective policing and the fencing off of IFP-supporting hostels. The ANC later reduced its list of preconditions to three.

Chip (formerly Don), 1992

During negotiations curious realignments of political parties and alliances took place. While Mandela and De Klerk were dancing a complicated tango, the Afrikaner right wing under Andries Treurnicht reached out to discredited homeland leaders like Oupa Gqozo, Lucas Mangope of Bophuthatswana and Chief Buthelezi, then still head of the KwaZulu homeland. They attempted to form a united front against the negotiation process.

Francis, Dugmore & Rico, 1993

The assassination of the General Secretary of the Communist Party, Chris Hani, was probably the most precarious moment of the entire negotiation process. For a few days it looked like the white right-wing's plan to de-rail the negotiations through inciting an uprising might succeed. But the right wing drastically underestimated the discipline within the ANC and the sway that Mandela held over the population. On the night of Chris Hani's assassination, Mandela appeared on television in a special broadcast, unprecedented in South African history, appealing for calm. Hani was buried a week later with great dignity, and the negotiations were saved.

Lou Henning, 1992

As the negotiations progressed, the IFP under Chief Buthelezi continued to boycott the talks. The violence that emanated from the IFP was of great concern to both F.W. de Klerk and Mandela, who are here depicted as listening to scary stories read by Buthelezi from a book entitled "Zulu tales and other scary stories". The story he is reading, loosely translated, begins: "It's dark, dark midnight, closer creeps the Zulu force."

Francis, Dugmore & Rico, 1993

In 1993, Mandela and De Klerk were jointly awarded the Nobel Peace Prize. Many in the ANC were critical of the decision to give the award to De Klerk at all, but most of the world saw the decision as an even-handed one which recognised De Klerk's decision to go, in Mandela's words, "further than any Nationalist had gone". Archbishop Tutu, a previous winner of the Nobel Peace Prize in 1984, was consulted by the Nobel committee and heartily agreed that the award should be shared. In 1999 Archbishop Tutu conceeded that in the light of what he had learned as the Chair of the Truth and Reconciliation Commission, he should have opposed giving the award to De Klerk.

Derek Bauer, 1993

The negotiations carried on for almost three and a half years.
Tens of thousands died – and the election of the new government
was still months away.

Francis, Dugmore & Rico, 1994

Nelson Mandela's autobiography, *Long Walk to Freedom*, appeared in 1994 and became an international bestseller. The book also became an essential accessory in households trying to show how in tune they were with the new South Africa.

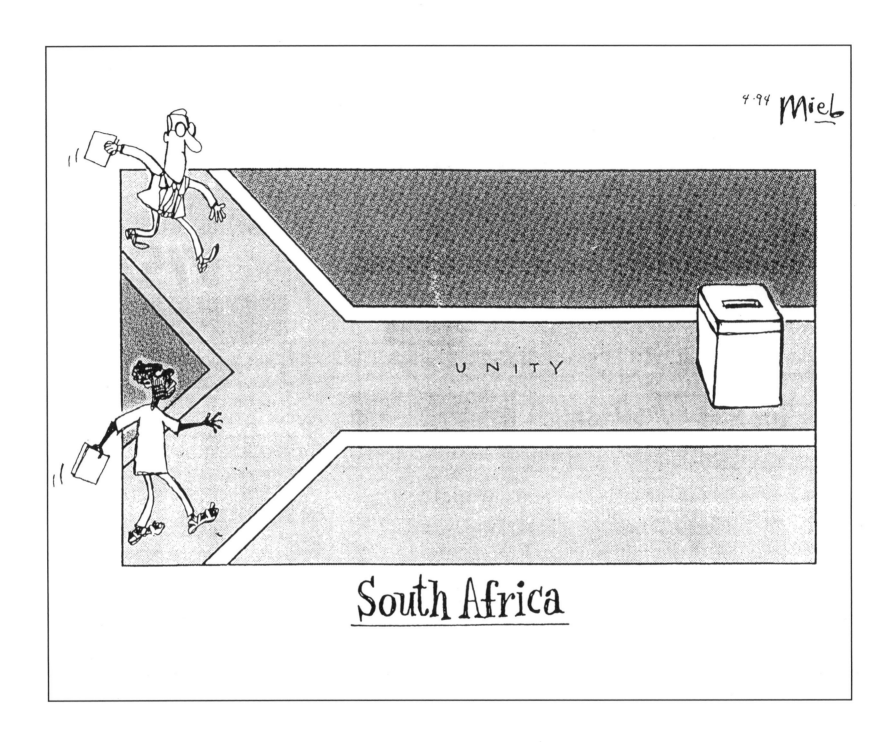

South Africa

Miel, 1994

South Africans of all backgrounds were now poised to vote together for the first time on the basis of universal adult suffrage.

Just before the election, the new South African flag, with its deep primary colours and unusual shape, was unfurled to great acclaim.

Chapter 6

Election and inauguration

Higgins

In June 1993, after three and a half years of negotiations, a date for South Africa's first-ever democratic elections was fixed. South Africans would go to the polls on 27 April 1994. Public reaction was mixed: black South Africans were generally jubilant but white South Africans were anxious and unnerved. Emigration increased sharply. A large segment of the white population were openly hostile to the elections. Eugene Terre'Blanche, leader of the neo-fascist AWB, whipped up crowds with his calls for the "Boers" to rise up and fight for their freedom. The call for a separate Boer *volkstaat* (homeland) was made with renewed ferocity.

In the run-up to the elections Mandela and the ANC faced three major obstacles: the potentially violent response of the white right-wing; opposition to the reincorporation into South Africa of the "independent" homelands; and the hostile stance of Chief Buthelezi's Inkatha Freedom Party (IFP) to both the negotiations and the proposed elections. Would these groups participate willingly in the new South Africa — or would they go to war to stay out of the process of democratisation? Dealing with these obstacles would require all Mandela's wisdom.

THE HARD RIGHT

The white right-wing had been fragmented for many years. Caught flat-footed by the unbanning of the ANC and other liberation movements in 1990, they took a while to regroup. But their opposition to black political rights was implacable, and when the election date was announced, it provided a clarion call for the white right to consolidate its forces. Retired chief of the apartheid defence force, General Constand Viljoen, suddenly emerged into the political limelight as the leader of a group calling itself the Volksfront, which was passionately opposed to the elections.

The ANC leaders, now part of a joint government with the National Party and other smaller parties called the Transitional Executive Council (TEC), realised that Viljoen's Volksfront was an organisation they had to talk to urgently and deal with seriously. At their first meeting, Mandela was blunt: he told Viljoen and his Volksfront generals that if the two sides went to war, the ANC would not be able to stand up to the Volksfront's forces on the battlefield. But he also warned that the right-wing would not win either, because of the ANC's overwhelming

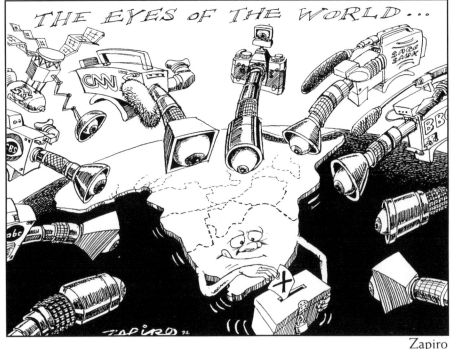

Zapiro

support on the ground, its impeccable international support and, ultimately, the ANC's superior moral cause. Viljoen agreed that such an inevitable military stalemate would be enormously destructive and would lead to the loss of many lives. An unexpected *rapprochement* developed: the two sides began to understand that they needed one another.

Viljoen nonetheless proceeded to argue for a *volkstaat* – an exclusive white homeland, which was so large (most of the old "Boer Republics" of the Transvaal, Orange Free State and Natal) that the ANC nearly walked out of the talks. But Mandela counselled patience: for the first time, he told the Afrikaner generals that the idea of establishing a *volkstaat* was not out of the question. But this could only be done if there was overwhelming white support for a separate white homeland. Viljoen demanded a whites only referendum to convince the ANC of the size of his support base, but it was so close to the date of the 1994 elections, Mandela said, that such a referendum was impossible to organise. Then Thabo Mbeki made an inspired suggestion: the right-wingers could test their levels of support through the election process itself. Thus was planted the seed of right-wing participation in the elections.

THE FALL OF THE BANTUSTANS

Another major obstacle was the refusal of the "independent" homelands to participate in the poll. Bophuthatswana, in particular, wanted nothing to do with the new South Africa. Bophuthatswana's leader, Lucas Mangope, insisted that his territory was an independent state – despite its landmass being divided into eleven separate pieces spread across South Africa, and the complete absence of diplomatic recognition around the world.

Then, in early 1994, history took a curious and violent turn. Bophuthatswana's civil servants went on strike, demanding the right to participate in the upcoming elections, fearing for their salaries after the election date (indeed many had not been paid for some months already). Mangope turned to his white right-wing associates in the Freedom Front. General Viljoen responded with alacrity: he quickly organised a "private army" of lightly armed soldiers to go to the assistance of the Bophuthatswana Defence Force (BDF). However, ultra-right-winger Eugene Terre'Blanche had also got wind of the request and, despite urgent warnings from Viljoen, issued a general call to arms. A large group of rowdy, drunken AWB members responded, and poured into Bophuthatswana. Rather than supporting their supposed ally, their random shooting of black bystanders deeply alienated the local populace. The Bophuthatswana Defence Force mutinied and began shooting back at the AWB. In one infamous incident, three AWB men lay sprawled next to their car at a roadblock, two still alive. A black BDF soldier screamed at them in a scene captured on television: "Who do you think you are? What are you doing in my country? I can take your life in a second, do you know that?" Then, as if to prove the point, the soldier shot the men dead.

The fiasco in Bophuthatswana sounded the death knell for Terre'Blanche and the AWB, and the white right in general. In the drama that followed, the TEC intervened by sending SADF troops to restore order. Mangope was told that his so-called country no longer existed. Shortly afterwards a demoralised Viljoen put pressure on the right-wing alliance to take part in the upcoming elections.

On 22 March, the leader of another recalcitrant homeland was forced from office: the Ciskei's Oupa Gqozo resigned as the Ciskei's civil servants also went on strike. The ANC leadership was jubilant: Communist Party leader Joe Slovo joked, "Two down and one to go." The "one to go" he was referring to was Chief Mangosuthu Buthelezi and his KwaZulu stronghold.

A ZULU MAVERICK

Buthelezi was Mandela's and the ANC's last remaining obstacle to long-term peace in South Africa. He had ordered his Inkatha Freedom Party out of the negotiations early on, in protest against the failure of the parties to consider his suggestions for a federal system – a system which would give considerable autonomy to his homeland. Throughout the negotiations, the ANC had manoeuvred as carefully as possible around Buthelezi, who commanded a large, fervent and armed following. Many innovative attempts were made to appease Buthelezi and bring him into the election. The Zulu king was even offered constitutional powers similar to Queen Elizabeth in the United Kingdom. When this did not work, international mediators including Henry Kissinger were called in, but all to no avail. Buthelezi wouldn't budge. His Inkatha Freedom Party were waging an escalating war against ANC supporters in both Natal and the urban townships around Johannesburg.

Buthelezi's last-minute request to have the election date moved so that further talks could be held was refused point-blank by Mandela and the ANC. This action finally seemed to have a sobering effect on Buthelezi. He realised that he was running out of options; if he chose to stay out of the elections and continue to wage war against the rest of South Africa, he could be captured and jailed or even killed. This was the grim but not entirely fanciful scenario painted for Buthelezi by his long-term friend, the Kenyan professor Washington Okumu, who made a last-ditch effort to get Buthelezi back into the election process.

ALL ABOARD FOR THE ELECTION

In the most last-minute of possible actions, Buthelezi agreed to contest the elections. The Independent Electoral Commission (IEC) would have to print eighty million special stickers to attach to the ballot cards. A special meeting of parliament would have to take place, the day before the election, to legalise the IFP's participation. It seemed like an impossible task but Mandela and the ANC insisted that it be done. Meanwhile many whites stockpiled tinned food, candles and water as they feared that either left-wing or right-wing groups would rise up in revolt and possibly cut off electricity and water supplies. The elections were looked upon with trepidation, as bomb blasts by right-wing extremists rocked the city centres. But with conservative Afrikaners finally coming into the election fold, the homelands reincorporated into a unitary South Africa, and Buthelezi finally joining the party, nothing would stop the elections now.

On 27 April, at dawn, the first voters began to arrive at polling stations to cast their ballots. White and black stood together in long queues, in the hot sun. For almost everyone, it was a day of catharsis, and of liberation. Mandela recalled with emotion in his autobiography:

> "The images of South Africans going to the polls that day are burned in my memory. Great lines of patient people snaking through the dirt roads and streets of towns and cities; old women who had waited half a century to cast their first vote saying that they felt like human beings for the first time in their lives; white men and women saying they were proud to live in a free country at last. The mood of the nation during those days of voting was buoyant. The violence and bombings ceased, and it was as though we were a nation reborn." ❧

Francis, Dugmore & Rico, 1994

Before the election, South Africa was beset with rumours and urban legends. White South Africans in particular were fearful of what the election might bring. Many hoarded food and candles, expecting some kind of apocalypse. This cartoon depicts the then popular rumour that once the ANC took power white-owned houses would be "redistributed" to black owners.

"YOU'RE FREE!... MIGHTY BIG OF ME, ISN'T IT?"

Gorrell, 1994

Some commentators and cartoonists had a very jaundiced view of
white South Africa's largesse in conceding to the election.

Francis, Dugmore & Rico, 1994

As election day approached, patriotic fervour and fear rose in tandem. As a security precaution, all voters had to dip their hands into a liquid, which was only viewable with ultraviolet light.

Various rumours floated around about the liquid – for example, that it could somehow reveal whom you voted for and that it wouldn't wash off for five years until the next election.

Zapiro, 1994

In his autobiography, Mandela describes voting for the first time: "Before I entered the polling station, an irreverent member of the press called out 'Mr Mandela, who are you voting for?'. I laughed. 'You know', I said, 'I have been agonizing over that choice all morning.' I marked an X in the box next to the letters ANC then slipped my folded ballot paper into a simple wooden box; I had cast my first vote of my life."

Zapiro, 1998

The election and his subsequent inauguration as South Africa's first democratic president have been the crowning achievements of Nelson Mandela's life. They fulfilled a mission that he had felt from a young age. As he recalls in his autobiography: "It was this desire for people to live their lives with dignity and self-respect that animated my life, that transformed a frightened young man into a bold one, that drove a law-abiding attorney to become a criminal, that turned a family-loving husband into a man without a home, that forced a life-loving man to live like a monk. It was during those long and lonely years that my hunger for the freedom of my own people became a hunger for the freedom of all people, black and white. I knew that the oppressor must be liberated just as surely as the oppressed."

Francis, Dugmore & Rico, 1994

Mandela's inauguration speech echoed the words of the great American civil rights leader, Martin Luther King: "Free at last". Even though things had changed dramatically in South Africa, it was clear that certain relationships, particularly economic relationships between white and black, were still going to stay the same, at least for a while.

Zapiro, 1994

The Independent Electoral Commission (IEC) took an inordinate amount of time to count the ballots, and the Commission was still counting until just before Nelson Mandela's inauguration on 10 May. Mandela recalled in his autobiography: "On the day of the inauguration I was overwhelmed with a sense of history. In the first decade of the 20th century, a few years after the bitter Anglo-Boer War, the white-skinned peoples of South Africa patched up their differences and erected a system of racial domination against the dark-skinned peoples of their own land. The structure they created formed the basis of one of the harshest, most inhumane, societies the world has ever known. Now, in the last decade of the 20th century, and my own eighth decade as a man, that system had been overturned forever and replaced by one that recognised the rights and freedom of all peoples regardless of the colours of their skins."

Zapiro, 1994

On Monday 12 May 1994, Nelson Mandela moved into the offices of the presidency in the Union Buildings in Pretoria. Previous white Prime Ministers and Presidents, Hendrik Verwoerd, B.J. Vorster, P.W. Botha and F.W. de Klerk, respond to this situation.

"FORCED REMOVAL"

Findlay, 1994

This cartoon shows F.W. de Klerk and his wife Marike being forced to leave "Libertas", the presidential home, as Nelson Mandela arrives downstairs. The reference to the notorius forced removals of apartheid gives this cartoon its sting.

Grogan, 1991

The ruins of apartheid. It does seem absurd – all the suffering, the twenty to thirty thousand deaths lost directly in the civil war, the millions of stunted lives, the pain of countless families torn apart by the migrant labour system, and the drawn out conflict.

Heng, 1994

Oppressed people throughout the world were inspired by the
1994 election in South Africa and by the end of 300 years of
white minority rule.

Zapiro, 1994

In this moving cartoon, Zapiro chronicles the milestones in Nelson Mandela's life. Mandela was always clear that after the election, hard work lay ahead. As he wrote in his autobiography, "The truth is that we are not yet free; we have merely achieved the freedom to be free, the right not to be oppressed. We have not taken the final step of our journey but the first step on a longer and even more difficult road. For to be free is not merely to cast off one's chains, but to live in a way that respects and enhances the freedom of others. The true test of our devotion to freedom is just beginning."

Chapter 7

The challenges of the rainbow nation

Reconciliation has been the central theme of Nelson Mandela's presidency. Unlike some of his harder-lined colleagues, Mandela has never underestimated the grievous psychological wounding of apartheid. From the mid-1980s it became clear that of all the obstacles in the way of achieving a democratic South Africa, a full-scale civil war was the most dire and, at points, the most likely. The hatred engendered by the spiral of revenge and retribution, attack and counter-attack in the late 1980s and early 1990s can ruin even prosperous nations. The tragic fiasco of the former Yugoslavia, the self-destruction of Rwanda, the wars between India and Pakistan, the 35 years of non-stop conflict in Angola, all of these point to what South Africa's fate could have been. It was Mandela's determination to seek the road of peace that would lead South Africa away from civil war.

Mandela had four major challenges to deal with:

- neutralising the threat of the white right-wing, and appeasing whites in general who might, as they did in Angola and Mozambique, take fright and flee the country with their much-needed skills and financial capital;

PRISONER, 1963-1990

- neutralise and incorporate the ethnic secessionist movement, Inkatha, led by Mangosuthu Buthelezi;
- control and channel the energies of the deeply alienated black township youth whose rage at the inequalities in South Africa and at the humiliations of apartheid knew few boundaries;
- forge a common sense of patriotism and nationhood without which no country has succeeded in the modern era.

This last challenge — getting people to believe in a new imagined identity, and getting them to want to contribute to the creation of a new South Africa — has been the single most testing challenge of Mandela's presidency.

Mandela had already gone a long way to achieving the basis for success in reconciliation in the four years leading up to the 1994 election. His incredible ability to empathise with people from all backgrounds, the ANC's impeccable moral argument, and the support of about 70 per cent of South Africa's population meant that he could command respect from enemies like Constand Viljoen and Mangosuthu Buthelezi. Pulling them both into the

PRESIDENT, 1994–

Dani Aguila

Zapiro

1994 election and thereby committing them to the rule of law, the parliamentary process, and the rewards of participating in the government – money, recognition, power – owed a great deal to Mandela's personal strategising and diplomatic efforts. Although the contributions of other charismatic negotiators like Cyril Ramaphosa, Thabo Mbeki and Joe Slovo cannot be underestimated, it was primarily Mandela who took the lead in winning over almost every section of white South Africa, from big business to the Afrikaner far-right.

By the time of the Rugby World Cup in 1995, the ANC's and Mandela's reconciliation policy was starting to pay huge dividends. The IFP had been partly pacified by inclusion in the government of national unity. The unpredictable Buthelezi had been largely co-opted and contained in government. Making Buthelezi the Acting President of South Africa when, on occasion, both Mandela and Thabo Mbeki were simultaneously out of the country was a masterstroke of nation-building.

Likewise, Mandela's special attention to the most conservative members of the white community has also paid off handsomely. The images of Mandela having tea with a variety of elderly white former racists, and of bringing them into the fold of the new South Africa, seemed to some to be a waste of presidential time. But breaking bread with the likes of Betsie Verwoerd and Elize Botha (wife of P.W. Botha) was part of a broader campaign to neutralise and allay white fear. By the 1999 election, the National Party and the more right-wing Conservative Party and the Freedom Front saw their election support dwindle into insignificance. The bogey man was gone – and in its place was the friendly and reasonable ANC of Nelson Mandela.

A LOST GENERATION?

Mandela's biggest challenge has been reconciling the more militant younger generations of black South Africans to the reality that economic liberation would be slow in coming. The so-called lost generation, shabbily education by apartheid's demeaning school system, and witness to the raw brutality of a long drawn-out and mostly urban war – have provided acute challenges for the new government. The government under Nelson Mandela has avoided the obvious temptations of wealth redistribution taxes, or the more drastic nationalisation of private white assets. Even land, so systematically stolen from black South Africans for the last hundred years, has been conservatively returned to black owners. White property rights, however illegitimate in certain cases, have been respected.

By 1999 Mandela had achieved many of his reconciliation goals. White hostility to the new South Africa has largely evaporated and white emigration has slowed down. Relations with Inkatha have improved to such an extent that violence in Natal can officially be said to be over. Black South Africans are slowly beginning to see some of the benefits of the government's economic policies, with entrepreneurial opportunities for blacks emerging in every sector of the economy. These may not be the hand-outs that some of Mandela's supporters may have expected but they are the basis for building long-term wealth and prosperity.

A LEGACY WITHOUT LIMITS

Given the challenges of what Mandela faced in 1994, the successes of his first five years of government are extraordinary by just about every measure. South Africa has avoided war and a nascent sense of nationhood is taking root. South Africans on both the right and the left wing of the political spectrum have learned a modicum of respect for each other's views. The economy is poised to begin to deliver tangible benefits to the poorest of the poor. There is much still to achieve, but Mandela has given South Africa a chance to join the pantheon of successful nations. The next five to ten years are going to be critical in determining whether South Africa builds on the start that Mandela's presidency has given us. ᕮᕬ

Makhosini Nyathi, 1994

The challenges faced by Nelson Mandela in his first months of presidency was the subject of many political cartoons. For someone taking over the running of a country with six million unemployed and a legacy of almost forty years of stultifying Bantu education, it was hard even to imagine where one could begin repairing the damage done by apartheid.

Grogan, 1994

Two cartoonists with an entirely different take on the same idea. Tony Grogan shows Mandela as the hero with sleeves rolled up who defeats the giant of apartheid and now has to tackle the relatively minor problem of crime in South Africa.

Zapiro, 1994

Zapiro also sees Mandela in a heroic role as the biblical David. Having now slain the Goliath of apartheid, Mandela has to face up to a much bigger threat – that of criminal violence in South Africa. Zapiro's cartoon has proved to be the more prophetic.

Zapiro, 1994

The ANC was at pains during its election campaign not to allow expectations to soar too high. Nonetheless, South Africa entered its democratic era in a euphoric mood with ordinary people hoping for a rapid rise in their living standards.

Derek Bauer, 1997

Crime would prove to be one of the new government's greatest challenges. Despite high-profile anti-crime initiatives, crime was the one problem that Mandela singularly failed to get to grips with during the course of his presidency. The overall crime rate continued to soar until it stabilised at unacceptably high levels in 1998. This cartoon depicts Mandela lecturing then Minister of Police Sydney Mufamadi and Police Chief George Fivas.

Lou Henning, 1994

Even after the election, sections of the conservative press continued to see Nelson Mandela and the ANC as merely a front for communism. In this cartoon, Ronnie Kasrils, Communist Party stalwart, is whispering to Joe Slovo, leader of the party, with reference to Mandela: "He is not going to make it for long, then you can take over the crown."

In the background, the "ghost" of the Communist Party is waiting in the wings and is also saying, "It's not long now, then I'll take over." Cyril Ramaphosa is depicted as the "second princess" in this particular beauty pageant, and he is shown thinking to himself, "Well, they are both fairly old", a reference to Ramaphosa's supposed ambitions on the presidency. Thabo Mbeki is tying a rope around Ramaphosa's leg. The little bird – a common feature of Lou Henning's cartoons – is asking, "Are these Mr [Kader] Asmal's beauties?" This is a possible reference to his perceived influence of an Indian cabal over the ANC.

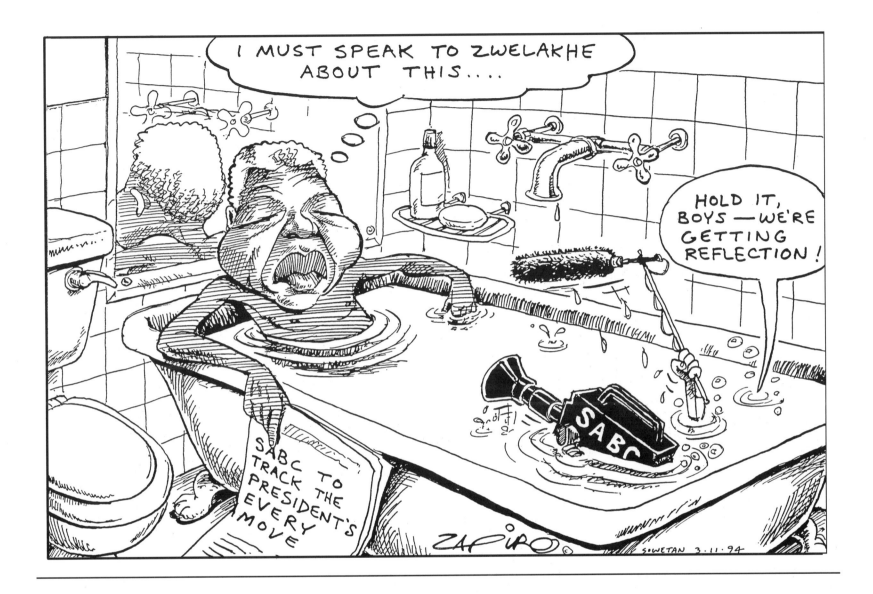

Zapiro, 1994

With the taking of high office came unending public scrutiny for Nelson Mandela. South Africa, the world and particularly the South African stock market clung on his every word: the prospects for South Africa's success were seen unfairly to rest on Mandela's shoulders alone. The "Zwelakhe" that Mandela is referring to in this cartoon is Zwelakhe Sisulu, then head of the SABC and son of Nelson Mandela's close friend and fellow ANC stalwart, Walter Sisulu.

Zapiro, 1996

Such was Mandela's perceived influence on the well-being of the country that even the smallest rumour about ill health could cause both local stocks and the South African currency to nose-dive.

The "Parks" that Mandela is talking to in the last caption was his publicity secretary, Parks Mankahlana.

Andy, 1994

One of the most interesting and complex challenges that Mandela faced was the wave of strikes in his first year of office. Workers, particularly government workers, expected a good deal more from the new democratic dispensation than they felt they were receiving.

Zapiro, 1997

Reconciliation was the by-word of Mandela's presidency. Going further than anyone expected him to, Mandela even visited Mrs Betsie Verwoerd, the octogenarian widow of the architect of apartheid, Dr H.F. Verwoerd. She was then living in *Orania*, a prototype whites-only *volkstaat* in one of South Africa's most barren areas. Mrs Verwoerd received Mandela graciously. By 1999 white Afrikaner support for the idea of an independent white homeland had faded into insignificance, partly due to Mandela's efforts to make Afrikaners feel welcome in the new South Africa. The sign in the background reads "whites only" And the coffee mug is engraved with the words "non-white guests".

Zapiro, 1996

Taking the reconciliation theme even further, Mandela became an ardent supporter of the nation's sporting teams. Mandela would drop in on the South African national teams just before a rugby, cricket or soccer game, to give them his best wishes. These encounters appeared to have an electrifying effect on the players. Here the Australian rugby team is represented by a flattened kangaroo: a turbo-charged Springbok team defeated Australia in the opening game of the 1995 Rugby World Cup.

Mandela's support for the almost all-white World Cup rugby team was a tactical masterstroke in terms of bringing about genuine reconciliation in South Africa. Mandela himself, like the rest of the world, was thrilled by the tense on-field encounter. "When it was 12 – 12, I almost collapsed," Mandela recalled. "I was absolutely tense. When I left the stadium (after South Africa's narrow 15 – 12 victory), my nerves were completely shattered."

Zapiro, 1996

Such was Mandela's effect on national sports teams, and their results in matches, a new kind of patriotism began to take hold in South Africa. The South African football team won the Confederation of African States (KAF) cup in 1996, and the national rugby and cricket teams continued to perform above expectations.

Francis, Dugmore & Rico, 1997

Mandela's effect on the sports teams and on ordinary people became known as "Madiba Magic". These cartoons imagine what might have happened had Mandela started believing the popular propaganda about him.

Dr Jack, 1998

The Truth and Reconciliation Commission was one of the boldest initiatives of the Mandela presidency. Although it was always going to be an imperfect process, the TRC has revealed the lengths to which the apartheid government was prepared to go in order to defend their system. Believing the maxim that the truth shall set you free, Mandela supported Archbishop Tutu's drive to reveal the truth about apartheid-era atrocities, without reservation.

Zapiro, 1998

The TRC started its work in 1996. Its brief was straight-forward: uncover the truth about human rights atrocities committed by both the apartheid government and the liberation movements in their struggle against apartheid. The process proved cathartic for South Africa. In Mandela's opinion: "All South Africans face the challenge of coming to terms with the past in ways which will enable us to face the future as a united nation at peace with itself. Ordinary South Africans are determined that the past be known, the better to ensure that it is not repeated."

F. Esterhuyse, 1998

A consequence of the soaring crime rate has been high levels of emigration, particularly by South Africa's white population. Mandela reacted with exasperation to what he perceived as a lack of faith in his leadership, and in South Africa's future. In this cartoon, he says "I can't believe that he is so unpatriotic that he would want to emigrate" -- referring to the barricaded South African citizen. Mandela was unrepentant about his remarks, calling into question the motivations of South Africans who could long endure apartheid, but now felt that the new South Africa had nothing to offer them.

Francis, Dugmore & Rico, 1995

A movie version of Nelson Mandela's life story is in advanced pre-production. Casting is proving to be challenging for the producers, and everyone is hoping that the merchandising strategy, if indeed there is one, will be more tasteful than that depicted here.

Francis, Dugmore & Rico, 1995

Imagine what Hollywood might do to the life story of South Africa's greatest hero. Maybe the idea of Wesley Snipes playing Mandela in a movie is not so crazy after all.

Chapter 8

Winnie Mandela

Befitting the Shakespearian hero that many see him as, Mandela's tragic flaw has been, in the eyes of his critics, his relationship with Winnie Madikizela-Mandela. His love for her ran so deep, and his dependence on her during his 27 years in jail was so intense, that a fairytale happy ending seemed inevitable. When Mandela was freed, so the story went, he would lead South Africa to democracy and he and his great love, Winnie, would be President and First Lady. But it was not to be.

LOVE AT FIRST SIGHT

Mandela was already married when he met Winnie in 1957. As he became increasingly committed to the struggle, his marriage to the deeply religious Evelyn fell apart. He was later introduced to Winnie by his friend Oliver Tambo. Mandela remembers: "I cannot say for certain if there is such a thing as love at first sight, but I do know that the moment I first glimpsed Winnie Nonzamo, I knew that I wanted to have her as my wife".

The very next day Nelson contrived to have lunch with her under the pretext of raising money for the Treason Trial. Thus began the forty-year obsession with his beloved and bewitching "Zami".

For Nelson's comrades in the late 1950s, Winnie was young and naïve. Winnie's family were uneasy about Nelson's involvement in the struggle and the fact that he was 16 years her senior. Despite these reservations Winnie and Nelson fell deeply in love and married jubilantly in the Transkei, a year after they had met, on 14 June 1958.

Their initial years together were marked by an intensification of the struggle. Within eighteen months, a state of emergency would be declared, and the ANC banned. Nelson went underground, becoming the renowned "Black Pimpernel". But the effect on his family life was more devastating than even he could have imagined – he dared not go home, knowing he would be arrested. By 1962, he was in jail.

In 1964, a mere six years after they were married, and now with two little girls, Nelson was sentenced to life imprisonment. In his autobiography, *Long Walk to Freedom*, Mandela frequently comments on how his love for Winnie lifted his spirits in his darkest hours and brought him countless moments of comfort. When he was released in 1990 Mandela said he was convinced that the suffering of his wife had been greater than his own. Indeed, in the almost 28 years Mandela was in jail, Winnie remained steadfastly committed to the struggle – and suffered systematic, sustained and brutal persecution by the South African security forces.

ATTACKING NELSON THROUGH WINNIE

Many people have wondered what went wrong. Why did Winnie's life take such ominous turns, which would eventually see her watching her former husband's inauguration from the sidelines, a rather sad and haunted figure?

Many have attempted an explanation for what turned Winnie from "a warm-hearted person into a mad creature", to use the words of Helen Suzman, the liberal lone crusader in

Zapiro

the Nationalist-dominated white parliament. There are many answers to this puzzle, but the rank brutality of the apartheid government seems to have made the most significant contribution to her growing loss of judgement and her increasingly erratic behaviour.

When Mandela was jailed, the South African government took a deliberate decision to "get to" Mandela through his wife. The police devised complicated webs to entrap Winnie. She would be betrayed over and over again by the networks of false friends which the security police deliberately planted in her life. She was also repeatedly harassed and detained, and in 1969 she was held under the notorious Terrorism Act, which allowed for indefinite detention in solitary confinement.

It was at this time that Winnie was subjected to brutal interrogations by one of the security police's most vicious torturers, the notoroius Swanepoel. Swanepoel was already implicated in the deaths of a number of detainees under torture. Winnie was tortured continually by Swanepoel and his team for five days and nights. Thereafter she was confined to a tiny cell, in total isolation, for over two hundred days. In all this time she was not allowed to bath or shower. Her lawyer, Joel Carlson, who was only allowed to see her after she had spent seven months in solitary confinement, recalled: "Winnie wavered between sanity and insanity, and never quite knew whether she would be able to live through her first period of detention".

After two subsequent show trials collapsed, the state resorted to other methods to abuse Winnie. She was banned for five years. During this time Winnie was arrested for breaking her banning order by meeting her young children for lunch: her banning forbade her to meet more than one person at a time. For this offence Winnie spent six months in Kroonstad jail.

All this mental and physical torture appears to have unhinged Winnie Mandela. Solitary confinement, especially for long periods of time, is widely regarded as a severe form of torture that can lead to post-traumatic stress disorder, depression and other changes in personality. Winnie's courage after detention remained undimmed, and in fact she took greater and greater risks. But the police kept up the pressure, and Winnie kept on being duped into befriending police agents, even allowing some of them to become close friends.

In 1977, in the wake of the Soweto uprising, Winnie was banished to the remote Free State town of Brandfort. Her house was burnt down and she was contiually harassed and taunted. Locked up on Robben Island, Nelson was as deeply affected as he was powerless to intervene in any of these atrocities. He felt personally responsible for her relentless persecution, which he had no doubt was designed specifically to erode his and his family's spirit.

Within the ANC, and on the ground in South Africa, Winnie gained vast popular support of her own. But she was becoming increasingly undisciplined and unpredictable, causing Archbishop Tutu to observe years later that about this time "something went wrong", with Winnie, "horribly, badly wrong". In 1988 the ANC formed a "crisis committee" to intervene in Winnie's "United Mandela Football Club", which operated from her home in Orlando West. The club was initially set up to protect Winnie, but for the Orlando community the activities of its members became increasingly more suspect. There were allegations of abduction, assault and abuse of adolescent boys and then the severe beating and murder of 14-year-old Stompie Seipei at the end of 1988.

In February 1990 Nelson finally walked out of prison holding Winnie's hand. Despite the keen desire of the world's media to portray a loving reunited couple, they separated in 1992. Nelson said in his separation announcement: "I embrace her with all the love and affection I have nursed for her inside and outside prison from the moment I first met her."

At the time of their separation, investigations into the murder of Stompie Seipei were still under way. While Winnie was charged with kidnap and assault, she steadfastly denied her involvement in anything untoward. Mandela too continued to believe in her innocence and supported her in every way he could. Winnie was eventually convicted on the assault charge, but her alibi – that she could not have kidnapped and killed Stompie because she was in Brandfort at the time – did not stand up to rigorous scrutiny.

Despite severe doubts about Winnie's integrity, the ANC decided she could best be controlled within the fold. Winnie was made the Deputy Minister of Arts, Culture, Science and Technology in South Africa's first democratically elected government. But her maverick ways continued. A high-profile love affair with a young black lawyer hurt President Mandela deeply, and her tenure in the cabinet was marred by scandal after scandal. Her estranged husband, the President, was eventually forced to fire her from the cabinet.

In 1996, Mandela finally cut the chain which had been binding him to Winnie and her antics since his release from prison. In the divorce proceeding, which Winnie desperately attempted to halt, Nelson resolutely and with great sadness formerly ended his relationship with her.

Today, as an ordinary member of parliament Winnie Madikizela-Mandela continues her life in politics, albeit with a much lower profile than the one she was forced to adopt during the past forty years. ೦೦

J. Morin, 1986

From the time of Nelson Mandela's imprisonment, Winnie Mandela was a thorn in the side of the South African security forces. No one denied Winnie's incredible courage and defiance in the face of almost round-the-clock security police surveillance.

General Hendrik van den Bergh, head of the notorious Bureau for State Security (BOSS), made it clear that every trick in the book would be used to harass Winnie in order to "stifle the political life out of this troublesome woman".

Lou Henning, 1991

Cartoonists have not been kind to Winnie. Here Lou Henning picks up on a news story that a circus artist had broken the world record of spinning 75 hula hoops. Winnie is depicted spinning a tyre, a reference to the notorious "necklacing" method of execution which she had publicly supported. Nelson Mandela is shown as having to keep many hoops going at the same time.

Francis, Dugmore and Rico, 1994/1995

Winnie was notorious for surrounding herself with a large number of bodyguards. In the light of the intense security police campaign against her for more than thirty years, Winnie's fear of harm from state agents may not have been misplaced. It was in fact a well-known tactic for the security forces to target the loved ones of prominent activists in an attempt to demoralise them. Nelson Mandela's friend, Ruth First, wife of South African Communist Party chief Joe Slovo, was assassinated by a parcel bomb sent by the security forces in 1981. Winnie was determined to protect herself but her zeal in this regard often caused ridicule.

Margulies, 1991

Winnie Mandela's life changed dramatically with the murder of young activist Stompie Seipei. The head of Winnie Mandela's notorious football club, Jerry Richardson, was tried and convicted for this murder, but he and others claimed that the order to murder Stompie came directly from Winnie Mandela. Although Winnie has always denied complicity in assaulting Stompie before his death or in ordering his death, she was convicted and sentenced to six years imprisonment for kidnap and assault. She later appealed against both sentence and conviction, and her jail term was reduced to a suspended sentence. To this day, police involvement in the Mandela football club remains a controversial issue, but more and more evidence suggests many of its members were police agents.

Chip (formerly Don), 1992

From the time of Mandela's release until his divorce from Winnie Mandela in 1996, hardly a month would go by without new revelations and allegations about Winnie's misdemeanours. "Disprin" is a well-known South African brand of painkiller.

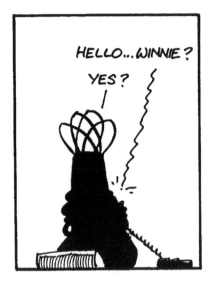

HELLO... WINNIE?

YES?

HI. I JUST CALLED TO TELL YOU NOT TO GIVE UP! REMEMBER... YOU'RE INNOCENT UNTIL PROVEN GUILTY! GET YOURSELF A GOOD LAWYER!

AND BELIEVE ME... I KNOW WHAT IT'S LIKE TO BE PERSECUTED BY THE MEDIA. IT'S A RACIST CONSPIRACY! THEY WON'T REST UNTIL THEY--

...LET'S GO, OJ! THE TRIAL'S STARTING!

ONE MINUTE! I'M ON THE PHONE HERE!

AND IN OTHER NEWS...

...WINNIE MANDELA DENIED ANY WRONGDOING AND CLAIMED PEOPLE WERE "OUT TO GET HER"... AND THAT SHE'S THE VICTIM OF A SECRET CONSPIRACY...

WHO'S WINNIE MANDELA AGAIN?

THE DEPUTY MINISTER OF ART, CULTURE AND SCIENCE FICTION.

MOM!!

Francis, Dugmore & Rico, 1995

Throughout the 1980s Winnie vehemently denied any wrongdoing. She regularly blamed various racist conspiracies perpetrated by either white or Indian "cabals" for her misfortunes.

The top cartoon depicts her talking to O.J. Simpson. The judge in Winnie Mandela's 1991 trial on a charge of kidnapping found that she was "a calm, composed, deliberate and unblushing liar".

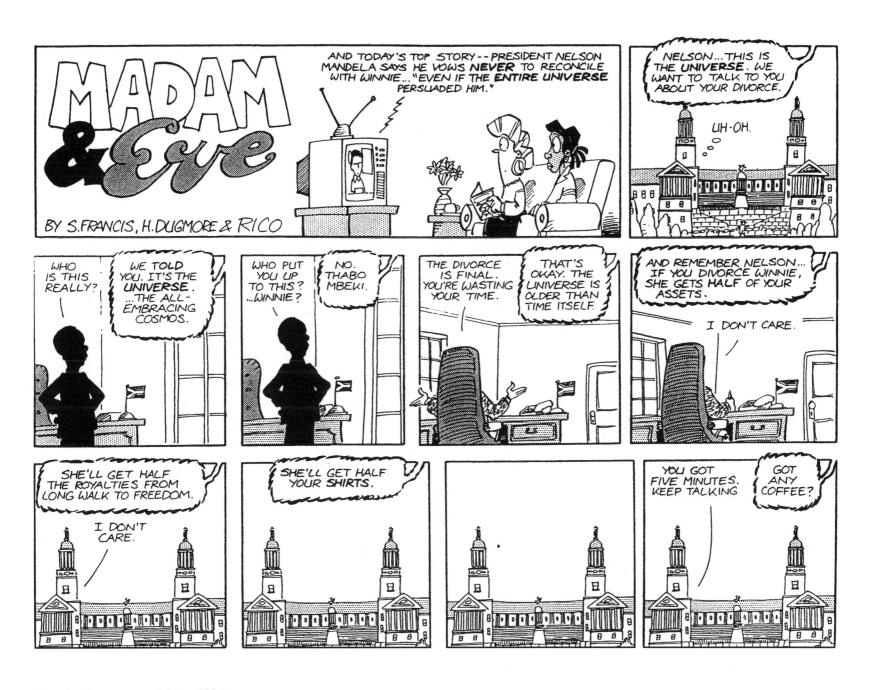

Francis, Dugmore and Rico, 1996

Such was Winnie's desire to prevent divorce from Nelson that she approached Nelson Mandela's childhood friend and nephew, Kaiser Matanzima, the discredited ex-President of the Transkei (the first homeland to be granted independence by the apartheid government). This infuriated Mandela, who said: "If the entire universe tried to persuade me to reconcile with the defendant, I would not. And least of all for Matanzima." Perversly, Matanzima not only was regarded by the ANC as a "sell-out" for supporting the apartheid system, but had also been Mandela's unsuccessful rival for Winnie's affections in the 1950s.

Zapiro, 1996

Once he decided to divorce Winnie, Nelson Mandela was determined to keep the legal action both low-key and discreet. Even though they had separated in 1992, Mandela waited four years to initiate divorce proceedings so that there would not be any confusion between Winnie's other legal troubles and the divorce action. Winnie was less reserved about commenting publicly about the divorce.

Findlay, 1995

As President, Mandela was initially a little surprised at Winnie's combative nature, revealed in both her political stances and her handling of their divorce action. In 1995, when attempting to fire her from the cabinet, Mandela said with classic understatement, "We must expect Comrade Winnie to fight back, but we have the situation under control."

MADAM & EVE

BY S. FRANCIS, H. DUGMORE & RICO

HELLO, MY NAME IS GWEN ANDERSON... ...AND I SUFFER FROM ... ≷CHOKE≷ ...WINNIE PHOBIA.

HI, GWEN!!

≷SOB≷

THANK YOU, GWEN. THAT TOOK A LOT OF COURAGE.

WELCOME PEOPLE, TO OUR FIRST DE-SENSITIZING THERAPY SEMINAR. HOPEFULLY, BY THE END OF THE DAY, YOU'LL HAVE CONQUERED YOUR IRRATIONAL PHOBIA OF WINNIE MADIKIZELA MANDELA...

AAAAH!!

SORRY. I USED THE "W" WORD... I APOLOGISE.

≷SOB≷ ≷CHOKE≷ ≷MOAN≷

OKAY. LET'S MOVE SLOWLY. I HAVE HERE A BOTTLE OF SOIL, TAKEN FROM YOU-KNOW-WHO'S BACKYARD. WHO WANTS TO TOUCH IT?

OH, COME ON! IT'S JUST A BOTTLE OF SOIL! IT WON'T BITE!

GOOD! THAT'S IT! PUT YOUR FINGER ON IT.

SPROINGGG!!

GASP!!

OKAY. SO MUCH FOR SHOCK THERAPY. LET'S LOOK AT THE VIDEO.

©RAPID PHASE - 1997 http://www.mg.co.za/mg/

Francis, Dugmore and Rico, 1997

Winnie became something of a *bête-noire* for much of white South Africa. Although a lot of her behaviour was unacceptable by any standards, it did play straight into white racial prejudice, and reinforced certain white stereotypes of "dangerous black politicians".

Chapter 9

International statesman

Dov Fedler

Nelson Mandela personified the crusade against apartheid and, more importantly for the rest of the world, against the very idea of racial superiority that apartheid embodied. He not only spent his life challenging racist ideas, but he eventually triumphed over them against great odds. He represents the ascendancy of law, rationality and moral wisdom over the crude, brute force of racism and apartheid. This has given Nelson Mandela almost unprecedented moral authority and made him a hero to the world.

THE IMAGE MASTER

Symbolism is a critical part of modern foreign affairs, and Mandela and the ANC have an intuitive understanding of this. Mandela's mastery of imagery is particularly powerful in an era of soundbites and snappy visual moments. Mandela's primary international goals have been to attract investment to South Africa, and to return civility to Africa. In conflicts ranging from the civil war in the Democratic

Republic of Congo (formerly Zaire), and the unending agony of Angola and its four decades of fratricide, to the issue of international sanctions against Libya, the ANC and Nelson Mandela have given foreign affairs their very best shot.

But Mandela's government's emphasis on the subtle diplomacy of quiet intervention, and its sometimes superficial reliance on imagery, have occasionally been naïve. The ANC did not always remember that in foreign affairs nice words and a big stick are often necessary to make a difference.

CONTRADICTIONS AND CONFUSIONS

It was in this context that Mandela seems to have been genuinely shocked when Ken Saro-wiwa and seven other human rights activists were executed by President Abacha, the Nigerian dictator, in 1995. Mandela had been working quietly behind the scenes with the Nigerian government, but to little avail. Similarly, Mandela's visit to Suharto's Indonesia did little to enhance the freedom of the East Timorese. South

Francis, Dugmore, Rico

Stidy

Africa has also been impotent in the civil war in former Zaire, and has been forced to embrace the new leader, Laurent Kabila, who is only a moderate version of President Mobutu whom he ousted in 1996. Similarly, all Mandela's moral persuasion has not impacted much on Angola, Ethiopia or the crises in Rwanda and other African hot spots.

NO INTERFERENCE

South Africa has also, curiously, taken a contradictory "we won't interfere in other countries' domestic affairs" approach to many nations. This approach always used to infuriate the ANC when it was applied to apartheid by the United States and Britain. But South Africa has used this same argument to explain Mandela's excursion to Indonesia and South Africa's swapping diplomatic recognition from Taiwan to China a few years ago. The one occasion that Mandela and the ANC did attempt to intervene with meaningful force in the domestic affairs of a foreign country – the 1998 invasion of Lesotho – proved to be unpopular and unsuccessful. Foreign policy is no easy walk in the late 20th century.

MASTERS OF WAR

Another weakness of South African foreign policy is its continuing arms sales to Africa. The new government inherited a lucrative arms industry from the apartheid regime. Instead of shutting this industry down, South Africa has, for example, sold weapons to both sides in the Congo war – a morally reprehensible position.

Although South Africa became the first country in the world to voluntarily end its nuclear weapons programme, and destroy the half-dozen nuclear devices that the previous government had built, the continued sale of arms to conflict-ridden areas does not create a good basis for being a real moral influence on world diplomacy.

PUTTING SOUTH AFRICA FIRST

Could this have been different? There is a strong body of opinion to suggest that Mandela has correctly balanced his internal priorities – reconciliation and healing in South Africa – while doing what he could in the rest of the world. This argument is based on the conviction that South Africa's influence in Africa depends primarily on South Africa's coming right in its own terms. If the South African economy booms, and if democracy flourishes, as it has done, and if unemployment and poverty are reduced, then Africa has a powerful engine to haul it out of its quagmire.

In terms of democracy, Africa now has an internationally recognised example to emulate. With the notable exception of Botswana, almost no African country has been able to avoid military coups or *de facto* dictatorships in the years following independence. Thabo Mbeki's trouble-free

succession to the presidency in 1999 in a free and democratic election stands in stark contrast to the "President-for-Life" syndrome exhibited even by South Africa's closest neighbours, such as Namibia, Angola and Zimbabwe. The relative stability and prosperity of South Africa is arguably its greatest contribution to the renaissance of Africa.

The cartoons in this chapter reflect the mixed record of the Mandela presidency in foreign affairs – occasional stellar successes, but also a more general malaise of inactivity and a lack of clear goals.

It is also apparent that the man who played such an influential role in ending apartheid could yet have a long-lasting impact in the world of diplomacy. Despite South Africa's relatively poor start, Mandela's success with Libya in the Lockerbie issue gives an indication of the way forward. As possibly the most natural statesman in the world today, and with his moral authority enhanced after five years as president of a complex country, Mandela may yet have more foreign policy successes out of office than he enjoyed when he was President. ☺☺

Francis, Dugmore, Rico

Zapiro, 1996

After the 1994 election, Mandela worked ceaselessly to win investment for South Africa from the world. As South Africa's most famous brand name, Mandela has devoted more time to encouraging foreign investment in South Africa than any other person.

Stidy, 1997

Mandela has always made a point of not forgetting his friends and the friends of the ANC. Even though Colonel Gaddafi of Libya was regarded as a polecat in the rest of the world, Mandela and South Africa maintained friendly contact and diplomatic relations with Libya. These contacts proved invaluable in bringing the Lockerbie crisis to an end when Mandela persuaded Colonel Gaddafi to hand over the suspects for trial in the Netherlands.

Zapiro, 1995

Although the ANC has proved to be a faithful ally to those who supported it during the long struggle against apartheid, there have been occasional lapses in this policy. The policy of the ANC towards the military regime of General Abacha of Nigeria was arguably too lenient. General Obasanjo's role in the

Commonwealth of Nations 1985 initiative, leading the Eminent Persons delegation, was, sadly, not reciprocated. Shortly after the publication of this cartoon, Nigerian leader and author Ken Saro-wiwa and six others were executed by the Nigerian regime.

Zapiro, 1997

Part of the reason South Africa is viewed as the engine for the African Renaissance – at least by South Africans – is that it accounts for almost 60% of the GDP of Africa. But another reason is the undemocratic and authoritarian nature of many of the regimes to the north of South Africa's borders. Mandela had to be extremely diplomatic in dealing with Africa's wide assortment of self-appointed rulers, military dictators and "Presidents for life".

Dr Jack, 1997

Many leaders have come to South Africa to bask in Mandela's luminance. Here, Laurent Kabila, new leader of what was Zaire, and is now the Democratic Republic of Congo, returns from one of his visits to South Africa with a little souvenir. Kabila has proved to be only slightly less corrupt than President Mobutu Sese Seko, the kleptomaniac leader of Zaire whom Kabila ousted in 1997.

IF YOUR POLITICAL CAREER IS ON THE SKIDS, AND YOU ARE IN DANGER OF BECOMING A LITTLE M...

....WHY NOT COME TO SUNNY SOUTH AFRICA, AND HAVE YOUR PHOTOGRAPH TAKEN WITH THE BIG M?

Zapiro, 1994

It's not only African leaders who sought to bask in Mandela's reflected glory.

Zapiro, 1997

In a complex and rapidly shifting world, some of the ANC government's foreign policy initiatives have not been well judged. In the light of the recent massacres in East Timor, and more than 30 years of outright brutality by the Suharto regime in Indonesia, Mandela's visit there in 1997 was arguably short-sighted. The visit gave unnecessary credibility to a cruel and oppressive government.

WHAT REALLY HAPPENED...

SORRY TO DISTURB YOU PRESIDENT MANDELA... IT'S CHIEF BUTHELEZI CALLING FROM SOUTH AFRICA.

TELL HIM THIS IS NOT A GOOD TIME. PRESIDENT CLINTON AND I ARE TAKING A PHOTO OPPORTUNITY FOR POSTERITY.

YES, SIR.

PRESIDENT MANDELA SAYS TO TELL CHIEF BUTHELEZI THAT THIS IS NOT A GOOD TIME FOR POSTERITY. THIS IS AN OPPORTUNITY TO TAKE A PHOTO.

PRESIDENT MANDELA SAYS YOU MUST GET OFF YOUR POSTERIOR! THIS IS A GOOD OPPORTUNITY TO TAKE LESOTHO!

...INVADE LESOTHO? OF COURSE! THAT'S BRILLIANT!!

TELL PRESIDENT MANDELA TO WISH ME LUCK! BY EIGHT OR TEN TOMORROW, LESOTHO WILL BE IN MY POCKET!

CHIEF BUTHELEZI SAYS HE WISHES PRESIDENT MANDELA GOOD LUCK. BY 8 OR 10, LESOTHO WILL BE IN HIS WALLET!

CHIEF BUTHELEZI WISHES YOU GOOD LUCK WITH THE PHOTO. HE'D LIKE A FEW 8 x 10'S FOR HIS WALLET.

HA!... AND PEOPLE WERE WORRIED ABOUT ME GOING OVERSEAS.

Francis, Dugmore & Rico, 1998

South Africa's 1998 invasion of Lesotho, which took place while both President Mandela and Deputy President Thabo Mbeki were out of the country, is another example of less than stellar judgement in foreign affairs. Chief Buthelezi was Acting President when the world was surprised by South Africa's invasion of its tiny neighbour. Maybe this is how it really happened!

Zapiro, 1996

Mandela's July 1996 trip to the United Kingdom was one of the great publicity triumphs of his presidency. Madiba-mania swept the streets of Britain, leading to many gags like this, as well as other cartoons depicting Nelson Mandela replacing Admiral Horatio Nelson on the top of the famous British landmark, Nelson's Column.

Carsten Graabaek, 1997

Nelson Mandela and the ANC have a great fondness for Europe and, in particular the Scandinavian countries which were ANC's most generous supporters during the struggle against apartheid.

Here, on one of Mandela's visits, his colourful attire attracts warmhearted attention.

Chapter 10

The sunset years

and finally...

Hello... and Goodbye!

Even as late as 1988, did anyone believe South Africa would change so radically before the end of the millenium? Who would have given credence to Nelson Mandela's prediction in the early 1950s that he would one day be South Africa's first black president? Those who have known Mandela for many years testify to his unwavering conviction in the justice of his cause, and his relentless determination to achieve freedom and democracy in South Africa. There is no doubt that his prescience is remarkable. It could all have been so different.

THE JUDGEMENT OF HISTORY

This debate about the relative importance of Mandela's own role versus the collective actions of the ANC will go on for generations. What brought about the South African miracle? The massive loss of confidence by international investors in the government of P.W. Botha and the refusal of international banks to roll over South African loans? Or the collapse of the Soviet Union and its socialist empire, which removed the sting from much of white South Africa's and the West's fear of an ANC government? Or was it the raw courage of prisoner 644/64 who, after 21 years of imprisonment, seized the initiative and unilaterally chose to begin persuading the government that majority rule did not have to be synonymous with catastrophe? This is the fascination of the past and of history – trying to decide on the most coherent explanation for the miraculous outcome which is the new South Africa.

Mandela himself maintains that he is nothing more than a humble instrument of the resistance movement, a "loyal and disciplined member of the ANC". He disclaims, sometimes with irritation, any suggestion that he is a prophet, a "Moses", a saint or a holy warrior.

But a surprisingly strong case can be made for the primacy of Mandela's personal role in liberating South Africa.

Chip

Certainly, the ANC may have thrown up other credible leaders – the calibre and depth of the ANC leadership in the past 40 years is possibly unmatched by any other African liberation movement. And certainly the repulsion felt for apartheid, even by the white government's allies, would have been no different. So the ANC could have managed these past 40 years without Mandela – or could it?

What is extraordinary about Mandela is simply this: he understands and has always understood that real change ultimately takes place in the hearts of people.

A MASTER STRATERGIST

From an early age, Mandela exhibited remarkable strategic gifts – in particular, an ability to argue a case forcefully and persuasively, slowly altering the perceptions of those around him. Mandela's own convictions and beliefs were never held as unchanging dogmas. The fiery young Africanist of the 1940s became a non-racial warrior for the non-racial Congress movement in the 1950s. As his biographer Anthony Sampson points out, Mandela has always been a master of imagery. Witness his role as a dashing young sophisticate of the 1940s, or the fearless volunteer in chief of the defiance campaign of 1952. Or the images of him, as the founder and commander of MK, in his guerrilla uniform in 1962. The years in jail added to what was already a legend, a larger than life aura that Mandela had long fostered. Why did he cultivate these powerful images of himself with such seeming care? Simply because it created a formidable opening for Mandela to move in and change the hearts and minds of those with whom he was dealing – including his most implacable enemies.

Mandela's appearance in his 1962 trial on the charge of leaving the country illegally is a perfect example. On the final day, when appearing for sentencing, he decided to wear traditional African regalia befitting his Thembu royal blood. The white warders were in awe, and when Mandela stepped into the court, the white magistrate was dumbstruck and apparently lost the power of speech for a minute or two.

Later on, in prison, Mandela's unwavering assertion of his own dignity, of his belief in himself and his cause, won over some of the most conservative racists within the South African regime – the prison warders of apartheid's jails.

MADIBA MAGIC

This charisma, later nicknamed "Madiba Magic" wrought a powerful alchemy. The ANC and Mandela had to create a vision of a new South Africa in which there was no retribution or chaos. They had to do this as much for their own supporters as for their white compatriots who had lived all their lives in a pervasive atmosphere of fear. Mandela worked on undermining that fear for well over 40 years. For example, he devoted a great deal of time in jail to learning Afrikaans, and Afrikaner history. His empathy with the white Afrikaners and their struggle against British domination in the 19th century was never forced or faked. This empathetic understanding of what it takes to change a person's deeply held mindset – and the neccessary skills such as good listening, the posing of plausible alternatives and the right mix of moral righteousness and firm principle – is what has set Mandela apart from most statesmen in the world.

From 1990 onwards, all this skill and charisma was used by Mandela and the ANC to out-think and out-wit the ruling National Party consistently and systematically. The ANC was able to do this, in part because of its incredible collective leadership, in part because of the huge support it commanded in South Africa, and in part because of the moral authority of its cause which Nelson Mandela had come to personify. It is this personification of a cause that made Mandela, as an individual, so central to the unfolding of the South African miracle.

A STATE OF GRACE

It is one of the great ironies of history that Mandela's very incarceration increased his wisdom, his ability to empathise, the subtlety of his argument and, above all, his moral and emotional authority. By the time he was released in 1990, it was clear that Mandela had achieved a state of profound grace – an alignment of his own deepest purpose in this world with the expectations of those around him.

Of the hundreds of symbolic acts that he conjured up throughout his life, and during his presidency, a particular highlight was the wearing of the Springbok rugby captain's jersey on the day of the Rugby World Cup final in 1995.

When Mandela greeted the players, as one recalled later, he actually knew who each one of them was, what position they played, and how they might individually make a difference on the day. Throughout the 1990s people have marvelled at how this octogenarian could remember the names of thousands of people across the world and, when meeting them, even asking about their families by name. This compassionate empathy, coupled with unprecedented moral authority, has brought nearly everyone around to Nelson Mandela's way of thinking.

And, after five years as President of South Africa, his compassion and authority are undiminished. Married for the third time at the age of eighty, Mandela's "retirement" is a scant slowing down of his determination to achieve real freedom, not just for South Africans, but for the unfree everywhere. As Archbishop Desmond Tutu has written in his foreward to this book, "Nelson Mandela is God's gift to South Africa; he is our gift to the world." 😊

Dov Fedler

Zapiro, 1996

Zapiro's parody of the famous Arthurian legend of the sword of Excalibur shows Thabo Mbeki – who had always been the ANC's Crown Prince destined to take Mandela's place as President – facing up to his competition. In reality, Cyril Ramaphosa, Tokyo Sexwale, Jacob Zuma and Mathews Phosa, although all prominent ANC leaders, never really stood a chance of succeeding Mandela. By 1999, it was clear that no one other than Thabo Mbeki had the qualifications, experience or credibility to fill Mandela's shoes.

Findlay, 1996

Following in Mandela's footsteps was not a prospect that any
leader could relish. Here, Cyril Ramaphosa and Tokyo Sexwale vie
with Thabo Mbeki to take Madiba's place.

Mogorosi Motshumi, 1998

Thabo Mbeki faced the daunting challenge of having to define his own leadership style and win his own place in the affections of the nation. The "Barker" and "Troussier" refered to in this cartoon were coaches of the South African national football team affectionately known as Bafana Bafana. Mandela was credited with inspiring the national football team to victory during these coaches' respective tenures.

Zapiro, 1996

Not too long after his divorce from his wife of 28 years, Winnie Madikizela-Mandela, Nelson Mandela began to be associated publicly with Graça Machel. Graça was the widow of slain Mozambican President, and staunch ANC ally, Samora Machel.

Mandela strove to keep their burgeoning relationship a secret, but the world wanted a happy ending to the Madiba life story and would not allow any hint of romance to escape unnoticed.

Francis, Dugmore & Rico, 1996

Not everybody was thrilled at the news that Nelson Mandela possibly had a new love in his life. Mother Anderson, the crusty old grandmother in the South African cartoon strip "Madam & Eve", took the news particularly badly.

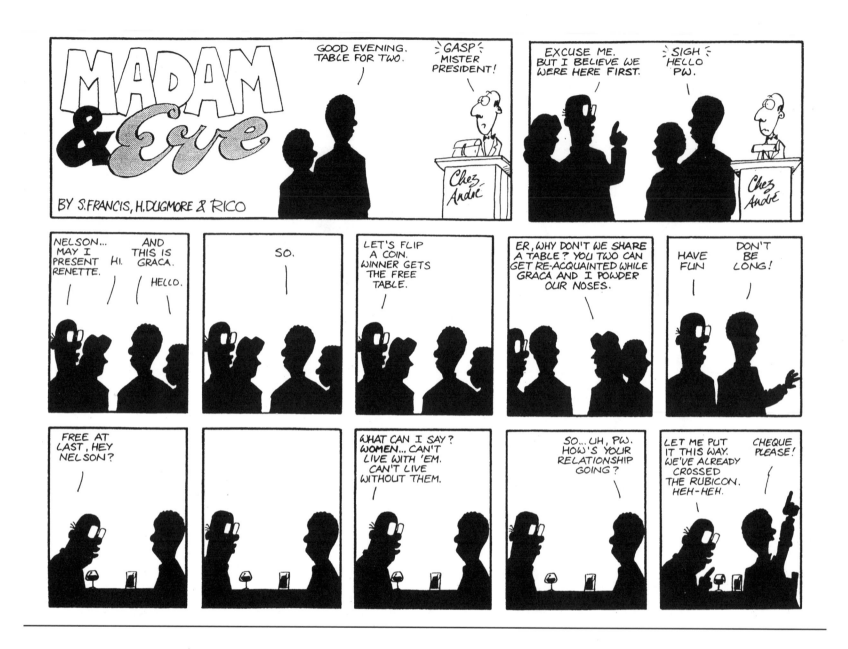

Francis, Dugmore & Rico, 1998

At the same time as Nelson Mandela revealed his affection for Graça Machel, his previous nemesis, P.W. Botha (now retired to an area known as The Wilderness, a scenic coastal town in the Cape), also began to go on dates again. Imagine if Nelson and Graça were to run into P.W. and his new "flame" at a restaurant. The punch-line of this cartoon refers to P.W. Botha's infamous "Rubicon speech" in which he adamantly refused to release Mandela and dared the rest of the world to do their damndest about his determination to maintain apartheid.

Zapiro, 1998

Nelson Mandela married Graça Machel on his eightieth birthday. As Zapiro aptly notes, it was possibly the world's worst-kept secret, but the President, and his press secretaries, kept denying the impending wedding until it actually happened.

Lou Henning, 1998

A more cynical take on Nelson and Graça's wedding, this cartoon is headed "South Africa and Mozambique made a connection on Friday". The guest with the invitation says, "I heard they got married in community of property", while the other guest responds, "Oh goodness, there goes the rand again". "Community of property" is a peculiarly South African marriage contractual option where the two spouses agree to share all the worldly goods they accumulate during the course of their marriage. Mozambique, as one of the poorest countries in the world, might, in this cynical parody, bring down the worth of the South African currency.

Zapiro, 1999

Mandela has always emphasised that he is not a prophet, just a humble servant of his people. But while that may be the case, he never shied away from the true test of leadership – daring to lead when no one else had the heart or the conviction. Mandela risked alienation from the ANC to take bold steps to break the decades-long impasse with the apartheid government, and rescue South

Africa from the grim spectre it faced. He recalled: "There are times when a leader must move out ahead of the flock, go off in a new direction, confident that he is leading his people the right way."

Zapiro, 1999

Mandela's humility explains a great deal about why he was able to
lead with unrivalled moral stature and integrity all his life.
"Aikona" means quite simply "No".

Zapiro, 1999

Living through the Mandela era, despite all the pain preceding it, has been an exhilarating experience for most South Africans. Mandela touched the hearts of his compatriots in a deeply personal way. We all felt we knew him, and continue to know him personally. It is rare to live through and to contribute to momentous and world-changing history. That is what Nelson Mandela, through his courage in the face of overwhelming odds, has allowed every South African to do. Nelson Mandela often cites the maxim of the great leader of the ANC of the 1950s and 1960s, Chief Albert Luthuli: "Let your courage rise with danger." Nelson Mandela has lived this maxim to its fullest possible extent.

List of Contributors

Dani Aguila, Philippines

David Anderson (aka Andy), South Africa

Bill Ashton, South Africa

Tony Auth, United States

Chuck Ayers, United States

Derek Bauer, South Africa

Steve Bell, United Kingdom

Clay Bennett, United States

Abe Berry, South Africa

Clifford Brown, South Africa

Peter Clarke (aka Graffito), United Kingdom

Bob Connolly, South Africa

Jeno Dallos, Hungary

Marco de Angelis, Italy

Kambiz Derambahsh, Islamic Republic of Iran

Bob Engelhart, South Africa

Frans Esterhuyse, South Africa

Dov Fedler, South Africa

Paul Fell, United States

Alastair Findlay, South Africa

Jules Feiffer, Israel

Stephen Francis, Harry Dugmore & Rico, South Africa

Gorrell, United States

Carsten Graabaek, Denmark

Tony Grogan, South Africa

Tom Halliday, United Kingdom

Heng, Singapore

Lou Henning, South Africa

Patrick Michael Higgins, South Africa

Thinus Horn, South Africa

John Halkett Jackson, South Africa

Mark Lynch, Australia

David Marais, South Africa

Marlette, United States

Miel, Singapore

Alan Moir, Australia

Jim Morin, United States

George Muller, South Africa

Jimmy Margulies, United States

Marlene Moultrie, South Africa

Mogorosi Motshumi, South Africa

Makhosini Nyathi, South Africa

Nyakanyaka (Aka Makhosini Nyathi), South Africa

Plantu, France

Jonathan Pugh, United Kingdom

Adrian Raeside, Canada

Len Sak, South Africa

Scrawls, United States

Shakespere, Australia

Richard Smith & Abbott, South Africa

Chip Snaddon, (formerly Don) South Africa

Nanda Sooben, South Africa

Ken Sprague, United Kingdom

Stacey Stent, South Africa

Anthony Stidolph (aka Stidy), South Africa

Jack Swanepoel (aka Dr. Jack), South Africa

Margaret Tabaka, Poland

Kieth Ticehurst, United Kingdom

Mynderd Vosloo, South Africa

Richard Wilson, United Kingdom

Zapiro (aka Jonathan Shapiro), South Africa

Suggested further reading

There are a number of excellent books about Nelson Mandela and his role in the struggle to liberate South Africa. Foremost is Mandela's own autobiography, *Long Walk to Freedom*, (Little, Brown and Company, 1996). Anthony Sampson's biography, *Mandela, The Authorised Biography* (Harpers Collins, 1999), is also a superb read, both deeply moving and comprehensive, and far the most definitive account of Mandela's life. Other useful biographies include those by Martin Meredith, (*Nelson Mandela, A Biography*, The Penguin Group, 1997), Mary Benson's *Nelson Mandela*, (Penguin Books, 1986), and Fatima Meer's *Higher than Hope* (Hamish Hamilton, 1990).

A number of other books provide valuable insights into Mandela's remarkable life. Allister Sparks' *Tomorrow is Another Country –the Inside Story of South Africa's Negotiated Revolution*, (Arrow Book, 1997), is essential reading as is Patti Waldmeir's, *Anatomy of a Miracle, The End of Apartheid and the Birth of the New South Africa*, (Viking, 1997).

George Bizos', *No-one to Blame? In Pursuit of Justice in South Africa*, (David Philip Publishers (Pty) Ltd, 1998), is a chilling account of the fight for justice in an age of barbarism. Tom Lodge's *Black Politics in South Africa since 1945*, (Longman, London, 1945), provided a good overview of the struggle for liberation.

Useful collections of Mandela's speeches and comments include: *In the Words of Nelson Mandela* edited by Jennifer Crwys-Williams, (Penguin 1988), *Nelson Mandela Speaks, Forging a Democratic, Nonracial South Africa*, edited by Steve Clark, (David Philip Publishers, 1994 in association with Mayibuye Books and Pathfinder), *Nelson Mandela's Speeches 1990, Intensify the Struggle to Abolish Apartheid*, (Greg McCartan, Pathfinder Press 1990).

The four cartoon collections of Zapiro, especially *The Madiba Years*, (David Philip, 1996), are one of the treasures of South African political commentary. Pieter Schoombee's, *Die Nuwe Suid-Afrika en Ander Liegstories*, (Tafelberg-Uitgewers Beperk, 1992), gives an interesting cartoon perspective on the recent past. Abe Berry's *South Africa and How it Works*, (Jonathan Ball, 1980), is wonderful look at the absurdities of apartheid, while Dov Fedler's, *The Season of Violins*, (1991), is an essential part of any visual history of South Africa. A masterpiece in its own right is Derek Bauer's *S.A. Flambe and other Recipes for Disaster*, (David Philip, 1989).

Various editions of *Best Editorial Cartoons of the Year*, edited by Charles Brooks, (1995), also contained some gems, although most of the cartoons are about America, with only a small international section.

Both the booklets *Selection of Anti-apartheid Cartoons from around the World*, (United Nations Centre against Apartheid, 1989), and *Drawing the Line, Cartoonists Against Apartheid*, (Anti-apartheid movement, 1985), were invaluable guides to those cartoons about the early years of apartheid.

Finally, Murray and Elzabe Schoonraad's, *Companion to South African Cartoonists*, (A.D. Donker, 1989), provides comprehensive, if dated, background to South African cartoonists and the history of cartoons in South Africa.